# TRIPLE WIN LEADERSHIP COACHING

## WILL LINSSEN

PASSIONPRENEUR® PUBLISHING

# TRIPLE WIN
# LEADERSHIP
# COACHING

The Coach's Guide to
More Impact, More Coaching,
and More Clients

## WILL LINSSEN

PASSIONPRENEUR®
PUBLISHING

Triple Win Leadership Coaching
Copyright © 2025 Will Linssen
First published in 2025

Print: 978-1-914082-14-6
E-book: 978-1-914082-15-3
Hardback: 978-1-914082-16-0

Due to the dynamic nature of the Internet, web addresses or links in this book may have changed since publication and may no longer be valid.

The author's intent is to provide general information to assist in personal development and growth. This book does not dispense medical, legal, or financial advice, either directly or indirectly. If expert assistance is required, the services of a competent professional should be sought.

The publisher is not responsible or liable for the content of this book or any consequences arising from its use.

**Publishing information**
Publishing and design facilitated by Passionpreneur Publishing
A division of Passionpreneur Organization Pty Ltd
ABN: 48640637529

Melbourne, VIC | Australia
www.passionpreneurpublishing.com

# TABLE OF CONTENTS

# WHAT OTHERS ARE SAYING

I am excited to share the positive impact our approach has had on coaches and leaders around the world. Over 4,000 coaches and more than 100,000 leaders have experienced the transformational benefits of using this methodology firsthand in their leadership coaching journeys. With hundreds of testimonials on my LinkedIn profile, I selected several testimonials to showcase the powerful impact our approach has had, providing real-life examples of growth and success for coaches, leaders, and organizations. We hope the insights offered by these diverse voices inspire and encourage you to embark on your leadership coaching journey.

## What Organizational Leaders are Saying

Having led organizations on three continents with very diverse leadership teams, it has become ever so clear that leadership is a personal and customized service that we provide to the people we work with in our organization. Working with Will helped me to cut through the complexity of diversity and accelerate my leadership effectiveness as I moved into a new leadership role. The overall experience has produced great insights and value for our business. Using the Triple Win Coaching approach from Global Coach Group provided me with specific suggestions from my team and other coworkers that we needed in our dynamic business environment to adapt to the rapidly changing requirements.

Will's expertise in leadership change and insights into our organizational culture helped me to swiftly and effectively pinpoint my leadership focus, and drive team engagement and empowerment at the same time. And as an added bonus, the transparent coaching process and measurable results made it all even more simple and enjoyable to create the change we needed for our leadership team. I have embedded this coaching approach in my leadership style moving forward.

Thomas Klein, Vice-President Mercedes-Benz

The challenges of leadership are exacerbated by the fast-paced, high-performance culture in our industry, which makes navigating all the people and leadership challenges more strenuous. GCG's coaching approach, where the involvement of coworkers is an integral part of the leadership change journey, was challenging at first but turned out to be the key to success. Taking the lead in change comes naturally to me, and the close involvement of my team and peers created a natural momentum that institutionalized the team and culture change when we needed it the most. This coaching journey has been a great win for me and my team, and has guided the business simultaneously. The return on investment has been amazing.

Simon Keeton, President ON Semiconductor

As a long-time CEO, I had the privilege of being coached by some of the best coaches in the world. Working with Will Linssen was transformational for me and my executive team, and it is clear why he ranks as the #1 global leadership coach. The last time I worked with Will was a really tough case. An entirely new management team, a difficult turnaround in a chaotic market, and a truly toxic culture. Will was super-quick to understand the details of the uphill battle we faced externally and internally. The agile GCG coaching process provided tangible guardrails for us to plan and make incremental improvements. It made it easy to commit to change and take one step at a time. Will also provided a wealth of frameworks and best practices for specific tactical and strategic projects we had been struggling with. All our leaders in the executive team got measurably better, and even our Employee NPS and pulse surveys improved significantly as a result. A great return on investment indeed. I won't hesitate a minute to work with Will again!

**Silvan Cloud Rath, CEO Twinner**

The coaching and leadership development program with Global Coach Group has helped me tremendously in becoming a more effective leader, which greatly benefits my team. Will brought a wealth of experience from different cultures, industries, and challenging situations. Throughout the coaching journey, he tapped very quickly into the issues that needed to be addressed and connected my specific challenges of a fast-paced, project-driven, high-tech industry with suggestions from my team and combined this with his experience into solutions that custom-fit my environment. Partnering with Global

Coach Group and my coach has been a great, enjoyable, valuable, and effective journey.

Dr. Eric Shero, Vice-President ASM

What Leadership Coaches are Saying

As a Harvard Leadership Development expert, I've witnessed the transformative effects of Global Coach Group's Triple Win Coaching methodology. This approach surpasses high standards and significantly enhances leaders' behavioral and strategic capacities. It fundamentally transforms coaching, ensuring personal growth, stronger teams, and improved organizational results.

Rajeev Mandloi, Harvard Business School Publishing

As an experienced coach and facilitator myself, I can honestly say that Will's expert-level knowledge of executive coaching, the application of that knowledge within a well-defined and structured coaching program, and the ability to support a cohort of distributed learning participants was nothing short of 'Master' level. During the GCG certification program, Will and the GCG team managed the online interaction with each of us, bringing his knowledge, supporting us in transferring that knowledge, and bringing energy, enthusiasm, and humor—it was a great experience. Will brought so much to the program that made the experience a fantastic one.

Adam Detwiler, USA

Unlock the true potential of professional executive coaching with time-saving strategies that set the stage for focused sessions. By streamlining the essential elements, leaders can dive straight into the heart of the matter, allowing for maximum impact and real results.

Cristian Hofmann, Switzerland

The Triple Win Coaching process provides a robust and clear methodology for coaches to utilize with so much 'done for you' in terms of client resources, templates, etc. For us, it formalized what we do as leadership and team development coaches, but importantly, it gave us a clear return on investment proposition to take to organizations, turning our coaching proposal from a 'nice to have' into a 'must have'. The combination of self-paced learning with plenty of practice offers coaches the opportunity to learn in their own time but also benefit from peer-to-peer work. Direct access to Will in the workshops was a huge plus as it gave us the opportunity to benefit from his vast experience and insight regarding the practical application of the GCG methodology. Highly recommended.

Helen Holan, Australia

Firstly, the program's philosophy of including coworkers in the leadership coaching engagement to improve their performance is a powerful tool to deliver behavioral change, and it has statistical evidence to back it up. Next, the coaching content was very strong and highly structured, giving the coach in training a step-by-step system to implement the various stages of the coaching approach.

Finally, the training itself was delivered by Will Linssen. Will is highly credible, engaging, challenging, thoughtful, and humorous, and he got the measure of the attendees and pace of the delivery just right. I would heartily recommend the program's training and Will Linssen himself to any executive coach serious about delivering value to their clients.

Jonathan Webb, UK

The Triple Win Coaching approach offers guidance and flexibility to provide a bespoke coaching journey for the leaders and optimally guide and support them in their leadership growth. It really helped me support leaders so that, in turn, they can achieve magnificent results for themselves and their teams. Working with the GCG's online coaching tools and resources in such depth has increased my capability and effectiveness to help leaders in their quest for growth and, at the same time, created a deeply ingrained connection with the GCG philosophy involving coworkers. Furthermore, the GCG process, system, and support allowed me to work on my passion for helping leaders achieve measurably improved effectiveness in a well-organized professional setting.

Marja Zandstra, Netherlands

# ACKNOWLEDGMENTS

This book is the result of encouragement from many people. First and foremost, I want to thank the thousands of coaches I have trained and certified over the years. Your dedication, enthusiasm, and commitment to excellence in coaching have been a constant source of inspiration and motivation for me and my colleagues at Global Coach Group. Without your commitment, community, and passion, this book would not have seen the light of day. I am particularly grateful to those who contributed to the creation of this book and the development of the Triple Win Leadership Coaching approach.

A big thank you to the leaders around the world who have entrusted me with their leadership coaching journeys. Thank you for your courage, openness, and willingness to embrace change. Your success stories have been the driving force behind the Triple Win methodology, and I am honored to have played a part in your leadership development and the success you cocreated with your teams.

I also extend my sincere appreciation to my colleagues and business partners at Global Coach Group who have supported me throughout this journey. Your insights, feedback, and collaboration have been invaluable in refining our approach and expanding our impact around the world.

A special thank you to the Passionpreneur publishing team involved in this book's production. Your professionalism, creativity, and attention to detail have brought this project to life, and I am incredibly grateful for your hard work and dedication.

Last but not least, thank you to my family for your unwavering support, encouragement, and understanding. Your belief in me has been my anchor through the ups and downs of this journey, and I am forever grateful for your love and patience.

This book is a testament to the power of collaboration, dedication, and the relentless pursuit of excellence. Thank you all for being a part of this incredible journey. Together, we are making a lasting impact on the world of leadership coaching.

# INTRODUCTION

Welcome to *Triple Win Leadership Coaching: The Coach's Guide to More Impact, More Coaching, and More Clients.* This book is your essential companion on the journey to becoming a more effective, impactful, and successful leadership coach. In these pages, you'll find the answers to your challenges as a coach and the tools to help you achieve remarkable results.

The purpose of this book is to equip you with the knowledge and tools to achieve the Triple Win: Better Leaders, Better Teams, and Better Results, with a 95% success rate confirmed by coworkers. This approach is grounded in the proven results from coaching over 100,000 leaders and their teams.

When I started my journey in leadership and executive coaching, I faced countless roadblocks and challenges that I wish I had known how to circumvent. This book is designed to illuminate those obstacles and share the hard-earned insights from my 30+ years of experience. I understand firsthand the complexities and triumphs of this field.

The promise of this book is simple: It contains the practical strategies and proven methods you need to navigate the intricacies of coaching and achieve transformative, measurable results for your clients time and time again.

The Triple Win approach is based on the foundation that 'Leading is Cocreating Change with Coworkers.' This philosophy underpins every chapter, offering you a structured yet bespoke approach to coaching that not only enhances individual leadership skills but also drives team engagement and organizational performance. By applying the Triple Win methodology, you will be able to deliver coaching interventions that are not only impactful but also measurable, bringing tangible benefits to the leaders you coach, their teams, and the broader organization.

In these pages, you'll discover proven techniques for creating smart beginnings to your coaching engagements, for maintaining momentum, and for achieving sustainable success. You'll learn how to measure the impact of your coaching, engage coworkers in the change process, and overcome common pitfalls that can derail progress. Whether you're a seasoned coach or just starting, this book offers valuable tools and insights to help you achieve better impact, better coaching, and more clients.

Prepare to embark on a journey whose every strategy, tip, and tool has been road-tested and refined to ensure exceptional coaching outcomes. Your path to becoming a more impactful and successful coach starts now.

# A NOTE ON TERMINOLOGY

**Leader:**   *The person being coached in a leadership coaching engagement. Some methodologies refer to them as a 'coachee' or 'client'. I do not use the word 'coachee', finding it awkward and slightly demeaning to a person in a leadership position.*

**Client:**   *The entity or person who pays for the coaching. Most of the time, that would be the leader's manager or the organization they work for. Sometimes, it is the leaders themselves.*

# CHAPTER 1

# ACCELERATE YOUR SUCCESS IN COACHING

## The most valuable tips and tools for coaching success

It seems like just yesterday that I started out as a coach. I vividly remember the insecurity, doubts, and stress I experienced during my first coaching engagement. It had come after many long working days gathering the resources needed to coach the leader, understanding their environment, and listing questions and answers that might come up. I had thought my transition into leadership development and coaching was going to be much easier, having already had the privilege of doing quite a bit of formal and informal coaching in my corporate leadership career. This experience had fueled my passion for helping people leaders improve, but when I finally stepped out into the professional coaching world, I felt the jitters of being a solo entrepreneur and the pressure to perform in my clients' corporate setting.

## DON'T YOU LOVE IT WHEN YOU THINK YOU ARE LAUNCH-READY, ONLY TO REALIZE YOU ARE NOT?

I thought my business experience and my MBA, recently completed at a world-leading business school, would suffice to get me started, but I was in for a rude awakening. Within weeks of starting my new career path, I was invited to be a main speaker at a conference on business and leadership, and as luck would have it, my first main coaching engagement came as a result of that presentation. The CEO of a large Fast-Moving Consumer Goods (FMCG) company hired me to coach him and his executive team. This was a mixed blessing. It was the sort of engagement any budding coach would wish for, offering high-level executive coaching at great fees—with the potential for fantastic references to secure more clients down the road. It also provided a great way to position myself as a coach within that organization.

The coaching engagement began in the span of a week, as the CEO was eager to get started with change in the organization. What I had hoped to be straightforward quickly became challenging. I had little experience in the intricacies of their FMCG business, and I was coaching a CEO I did not know well. I didn't know his team either, or the intricacies of this business environment.

I was reminded of something my manager and CEO had told me a few years back: Oftentimes doctors use a medicine they know something about, against a medical issue they know little about, for a patient they know nothing about. That's exactly how I felt, and I did not want to be that kind of service provider to my clients.

With little time to waste, I jumped into full gear. When you're coaching someone in a situation with so many unknowns, the biggest challenge is to determine which coaching resources to use. How could I add value to their environment? That was a tough question.

## BATTLING IMPOSTER SYNDROME WITH BETTER INSIGHT

For the first time in my professional career, I encountered challenges like Imposter Syndrome and questioned whether I was the right partner for this leader and his team. Failure was not an option, and I really wanted to deliver great value for my first client. So, for days, I worked tirelessly behind my desk to gather relevant resources and read up on developments in the client's particular industry and environment. I wanted to become a valuable and relevant discussion partner for the CEO. Armed with some of that information and a bunch of questions, I dove headfirst into the coaching engagement and vowed to sort things out along the way.

I dipped into my network of connections in the United States (USA), United Kingdom (UK), and India and conducted a rapid-fire round of interviews with experienced coaches and consultants to get their views on how they would approach this. I started combining my experience with their advice on different assessment tools, which proved to be a blessing. These tools provided insights into the leader's effectiveness, at least as seen by their coworkers, and this 360-degree method helped me establish a structure for my approach. I also gathered valuable information and examples by interviewing the leader and their executive team; I asked questions about their strengths, areas for development, and organizational challenges from a cultural and leadership perspective.

That approach relieved my performance anxiety and resolved the initial challenges I saw in front of me.

## DEVELOPING A BESPOKE SERVICE OFFERING

With the first big challenges sorted out, I had a few weeks to determine the appropriate bespoke service offering to help the leader make progress. Little did I know that this seemingly straightforward task would pose a whole new set of challenges.

Every day felt like a race against time. The leader needed to feel and see their improvement quickly, and I needed to facilitate this success and make it visible to them. The stress was palpable, and I felt the weight of their expectations pressing down on me—and my one chance to achieve success.

With just enough time before diving into the weeds of coaching implementation, I traveled to the USA and the UK to become certified in various coaching tools and approaches. I was committed to fortifying my coaching service, fearing that I might not be enough. While these certifications provided useful ideas and resources, they also opened the door to another set of problems. How would I combine these tools to create a logically structured coaching service and create the impact that my first client was looking for?

It was not the ideal start I had envisioned, and with no grace period, I resorted to many late nights working on the coaching program design. I remember putting my children to bed and then burning the midnight oil using the computer in their room to print coaching session materials while refining coaching techniques at my desk in another room. Every day, I repeated to myself that I only needed to stay two steps ahead of my very smart client and work through the rest along the way. But the bouts of panic and doubt that crept back week after week were relentless.

Each day felt like a marathon of blood, sweat, and tears. Yet, despite the exhaustion and the constant fear of failure, the first engagement went well and yielded great results. This success led to more engagements within the same company. However, I quickly realized that this 'improve as you move' approach was neither sustainable nor scalable. Psychologically and physically taxing, it threatened to drain the fun and passion from my newfound career path.

I needed a more structured, scalable approach to coaching to make it sustainable. The initial success was a testament to my determination, but the journey was fraught with anxiety and sleepless nights. This experience underscored the importance of having a robust and well-thought-out coaching framework to prevent burnout and ensure long-term success.

## USING A MODULAR APPROACH THAT PRODUCES MEASURABLE RESULTS

During my first five engagements, completed in the first 18 months of my new career, my process engineering and business background helped me articulate and address the three main challenges to making my coaching practice a success.

- First, lacking clarity and repeatability, I created a defined service proposition, developed modular coaching tools and resources, and focused on the measurability of results. Essentially, I combined two famous adages: You can only manage what you can measure, and What gets rewarded gets repeated.

- Second, having determined to use modular resources, I thought that more coaching training certifications would provide ready-to-go resources for use with clients. That was not the case, and frankly, this was quite disappointing. Many years later, I have completed more than 15 different certifications in various assessment tools and coaching techniques. Each of these certifications has contributed to my development as a coach, but I have always needed to do a lot of work to adapt the materials for use with clients. I found it odd and frustrating that after all that costly learning, I needed to spend my valuable time creating resources to work with clients. Investment in coaching certifications should translate into saving time in preparation.

I vowed to myself that when I started training coaches myself someday, they would get what they needed to coach. It should be like, 'Get certified today and use your ready-made resources to start coaching your first client tomorrow!' I wanted people who worked with me to get:

- All the training and practice needed to be comfortable starting their first paid engagement with a client (and start capitalizing on their investment in the certification).

- All the necessary resources that coaches can use immediately with their clients, thus saving the coach valuable time and resources.

- Commercial insights into running their coaching practice, including sales, agreements, and fee structures they can use with clients.

As my coaching business grew and coaches became interested in my approach, I developed my coach training business in parallel. Over the years, it evolved into the largest leadership coaching network in the world, currently known as Global Coach

Group. What we have implemented in our coaching certification programs is what some coaches refer to as 'a coaching business in a box'—everything you need to be successful as a leadership coach.

- Third, I needed data, so I began to measure results that matter. Clients understandably compare coaching to other professional services they use, like consulting or legal services, and results become a part of the conversation. Questions arise about the benefits coaching provides to the leader, their team, and their performance. Obviously, they want to assess the return on investment, which is a usual part of their business. Even though it was difficult to answer such questions, I felt a moral responsibility to address them, having been on the other side of that discussion for many years.

When it comes to this third challenge, many in the coaching industry cite confidentiality and the difficulty in measuring results to direct conversations with clients away from results. I never considered this to be acceptable. In my early days working in IT systems development for supply chain management in the early nineties, similar issues were raised about implementing these systems in organizations. Back then, we used a combination of quantitative results and qualitative benefits to justify the investment.

Armed with that concept, I explored the issue, coming across the work of people like Dr. Rensis Likert, Dr. Robert Cooke, and Dr. Daniel Goleman, who made tremendous efforts in measuring the effectiveness of behaviours and connecting these behaviors to quantitative and qualitative outcomes for the organization. Separately, Marshall

Goldsmith applied a focused mini-survey measuring coworkers' perceptions of behavior change.

Their work inspired me to adopt a similar approach. I integrated their methodology into our coaching practice, which led to the creation of our pulse survey. At first, it only measured the improvement of the leader, but over time we included the improvement of the team's effectiveness and organizational performance, all as observed by coworkers. While applying this approach seemed risky, I believed it was necessary for me as a coach to put my money where my mouth was and demonstrate the value of coaching through measurable outcomes as observed by coworkers.

We have continuously refined our coaching approach and now boast a 95% success rate of coworkers acknowledging improvements in the leader, the team, and overall performance results. I am very grateful for the inspiration from the great minds mentioned earlier, who often personally encouraged me to apply their approaches to my coaching.

## WHEN LEADERS AND THEIR MANAGERS UNDERMINE THE COACHING

After three years and two dozen or so engagements, I had a good process figured out—a clearly defined service proposition with modular coaching tools and related resources focused on measurable results that I could even guarantee.

With the coaching service flow and resources figured out, I thought everything would come off without a hitch. What else could stand in the way? I certainly couldn't imagine leaders or their managers being the problem. During my professional career, I had always worked with leaders eager to learn and become better managers. Now, as a coach, I naturally assumed leaders would enjoy being coached and getting better for themselves and the people in their team.

I had another rude awakening: Coachability could be a big stumbling block. I tripped over it during an early coaching engagement. The company had sponsored the coaching of one of their leaders, but, as I eventually learned, the leader did not really want to be coached. Their lack of progress stumped me at first. Why would someone who agreed to coaching not want to get better? Because that's what coaching is aiming for, right? I started doubting my coaching approach and resources. Were they not good enough, even though they had produced great results with others?

Action plans were not followed through on, despite the leader telling me otherwise. It was not a problem that appeared in one particular coaching session. It was more like clouds gathering over a couple of months; then, all of a sudden, lightning struck the coaching journey and brought all to a screeching halt. After a deeper dialogue with the leader, it became clear that they had more or less been forced into this coaching by their manager. This was not something that I, as a coach, was inherently in a position to solve. What resources could I create? What coaching services could I design? How could I make a leader engage in their own leadership change and ensure they implemented their action plans?

I wanted to help the leader as well as their manager and the broader organization, so I considered diving deeper into the organization and spending more time with the manager and coworkers to help the leader implement their action plans. But I realized that would be just wrong: Taking over leadership activities and responsibilities from the leader is contrary to what the coaching aims for. Additionally, such an option would obviously take a lot of extra time, which had no hope of being compensated.

# WHAT GETS IN THE WAY OF COACHABILITY?

It took me some time to figure out this coachability problem, because a number of variations of it had surfaced over various coaching engagements. As I was getting my head around this issue, I recalled a remark Stephen Covey had made in a program I had attended with him. It had to do with teaching and changing people; he said:

> Though we can help everybody, not everybody wants to be helped. As a teacher we should not focus on the ones who need our help the most, but on the ones who want our help the most. The more we help the people who want our help the most, the more impact we make and the more other people will come around for our help.

These words kicked off the journey to the solution. The pivotal question is, 'Which leaders are coachable and which leaders are not coachable?'

It turns out that there is much more to that question than meets the eye, because coachability can be impacted by the leader, their manager, or other coworkers. In my coaching journey, I've encountered a number of variations of coachability challenges. I discuss them in Chapter 4 ('Start Smart'), where you will discover the importance of determining coachability through commitment-oriented pre-engagement questions and creating a clear understanding of intentions and the level of commitment from all parties. In that chapter, you can learn about a unique coaching tool designed to solidify leaders' commitment to growth; we'll also explore solutions that generate momentum and forge a more fulfilling coaching experience for everyone involved.

## GETTING LEADERS UNSTUCK

Excitement and momentum are essential in every successful coaching engagement; however, during a 6 to 12-month engagement, leaders can get stuck in their change journey for various reasons. I have analyzed these situations and looked to successful coaching engagements to identify key differences. Common reasons for getting stuck include interferences arising from significant organizational change or challenges in one's personal life; feeling that change requires too much work without fast results; perceiving a lack of collaboration from coworkers; and declaring victory too early for the change to take hold.

At the same time, I noted some common traits of leaders who successfully completed the coaching with glorious results. They tend to maintain focus on the big picture, crowdsource challenges and solutions, and remain committed to the promises they make. With these insights, I reverse-engineered several tools to help leaders get unstuck, including the Triple Win Business Case, and a commitment to cocreating change with coworkers.

A number of solutions can be used early in the coaching engagement. Coaches can then effectively remind leaders of their own strategies when they face challenges, helping them stay committed and motivated. These are de facto evergreen solutions that remain valid throughout the coaching engagement. You can find out more about these coaching tools to keep the change momentum going and unlock leadership potential in Chapters 5 (A Committed Start), and 6 (Focus Changes Everything), and 9 (Leveraging Challenges).

The frustration and stress I felt when I started my coaching journey faded over time. The bigger picture began coming together, eureka moments morphing into a coaching methodology and measurable results becoming the bedrock of the coaching approach. This would later evolve into the current Triple Win Leadership Coaching approach. But we were not there just yet. With more clients and coaches interested in this results-driven approach to coaching, in 2012, I went all in and heavily invested in training and certifying coaches in this approach.

I wanted to spare new coaches the challenges and frustrations I had felt. Time and energy should be spent on helping leaders get better and not reinventing the proverbial wheel. I set one central objective for the coaching certification that I wished others had provided for me: Coaches certified today should be able to coach their first client tomorrow!

And so I set about providing all the principles I outlined, that is: all the training and practice a coach needs for their first paid engagement with a client; all the resources they need to get started; and the commercial insights they'd need to run their coaching practice. I added people to my team and we got to work developing resources and technology. Pioneering with eLearning and online coaching tools was one of the challenges we took on in 2013.

Reflecting upon my twenty-five-year coaching journey, I can say that it's much easier to connect the dots in retrospect than it was to attempt to connect them while looking ahead. But this is what I have learned on my journey:

- More structure using a defined service proposition creates more freedom to use a modular approach and customize the coaching engagement along the way.

- Involving coworkers in the coaching journey makes coaching more relevant for the leader and more hands-on for the coach.

- It also makes measuring and guaranteeing results a lot more reliable.

- It is not about the coach but about the leader and their coworkers.

# ROAD-TESTED AROUND THE WORLD

What I'm going to share with you in this book has been road-tested with over a million leaders and their coworkers. We have data on more than 100,000 leaders using this coaching approach. Considering the important leadership metric of leaders improving their effectiveness in the eyes of their coworkers, our coaching has shown a 95% success rate. With 98% of leaders being satisfied with their coaching journey, we can guarantee they will achieve results. So, if you aim to be a coach who hits the bullseye 95% of the time, has 98% of leaders incredibly grateful for guiding them on their journey, and is confident in guaranteeing that leaders will obtain the results they're seeking, you will enjoy reading this book. On the other hand, if your approach to coaching primarily involves supporting leaders by only raising their awareness and creating an initial action plan while downplaying the leaders' coworker interaction and getting measurable results, be prepared for a paradigm shift as you delve into this book.

With more than 30 years of experience in organizational leadership and coaching in North and South America, Europe, Asia, Australia, and Africa, and with more than 20,000 coaching hours on the clock, I can say with confidence that everything in this book works with leaders at any level, in any organization, in any country and culture, and in any industry—provided these leaders really care about themselves, their teams, and their organizational performance.

This approach has been used with more than a million leaders around the world. As we all know, ego is not something that helps a coach in their business, yet it is satisfactory to see that all this work has been worth it. I have been recognized as the LinkedIn Executive Coaching Top Voice, the #1 leadership coach in the world by Global Gurus (USA), and the #1 coach trainer by Thinkers50 (UK). I am an advisor to the *Harvard Business Review* and have been accredited at the highest level by the International Coaching Federation as a Master Certified Coach.

This book is for ambitious coaches who want to help results-driven leaders achieve a Triple Win: to improve themselves, make a positive difference in engaging their team, and enhance their business performance. The Triple Win delivers Better Leaders, Better Teams, and Better Results, and it helps you as a coach to have more impact, more coaching, and more clients. This reinforcing cycle will accelerate your success even more.

## ELEARNING RESOURCES

Chapter resources and demos are available in your eLearning account. Sign up and access it here: www.globalcoachgroup.com/triplewinbook or email coach@globalcoachgroup.com

# CHAPTER 2

# UNVEILING THE BLUEPRINT FOR COACHING SUCCESS

The most valuable tips and tools for
Triple Win Leadership

I remember sitting in a Silicon Valley office, coaching the CEO of a rapidly growing startup company. We were discussing his approach to learning. This is what he said:

> *Will, learning from one's mistakes is expensive, time-consuming, and painful. And as we traverse through the treacherous landscape of business and life, I very quickly learned two things. As human beings, we cannot possibly afford the time or financial burden of experiencing all mistakes firsthand. Instead, we can spare ourselves tremendous time, money and pain by absorbing learnings from the mistakes of others who have walked that path before us.*

With each word etched upon the pages of this book, I am compelled to share the invaluable experience I have gained throughout decades of coaching. It is a reservoir of knowledge derived from working with thousands and thousands of leaders and coaches from around the globe. It has awakened in me a fervent drive to help others find their way to success quickly, just as I was fortunate enough to find mine.

The knowledge and experience in this book will help you accelerate your path to coaching success. It is also designed to enable you to add your own coaching approaches to it—to infuse your passion into the coaching service you provide to your clients.

Allow me to share something I learned very early in my coaching journey. What clients want from coaching is results. They don't just want to hear from the leader that they improved; clients want to hear from the leader's team, manager, and other coworkers that they are satisfied with the leader's improvement. They want to see how it has improved the team's effectiveness and impacted performance results. Clients want tangible evidence.

That continuous chorus from clients started my quest to offer a coaching service that delivers on these client needs. That is how Triple Win Leadership Coaching came into existence: a crafting of services intended to help the leader improve their own effectiveness and their team's effectiveness, while moving the needle on performance. A collective effort with coworkers is a key element for making this service a success.

The journey to our approach included learning from others in a very broad sense, for example, from approaches to behavioral change already prevalent in coaching or practiced in other areas within organizations. As time went by, this resulted in better results than we could have imagined. We actually checked the numbers over and over again to confirm their accuracy and the efficacy of the coaching service. As mentioned in Chapter 1, the coaching approach consistently produced a 95% success rate. This is now known as our Triple Win Leadership Coaching – Better Leaders, Better Teams, Better Results, with a 95% success rate confirmed by coworkers.

What are the coaches getting from this approach? I've talked to thousands of them over the years, and they generally want more clients and to gain more coaching expertise. And their clients have the same results-based requirements. So, to get more clients and do more coaching, coaches need to be able to create more impact with their clients. And this is precisely how Triple Win Leadership Coaching benefits the coach. Coaches, using my Triple Win

Coaching approach, deliver a Triple Win for the client. They create more impact and do more coaching with clients who love the progress they are making. And because the coaching produces stellar results, they can get more coaching engagements with the same clients and other clients. Triple Win Leadership Coaching means more impact, more coaching, and more clients.

## MAKE YOUR WORTH WORTH IT

Right from the start of my coaching career, it was clear that the main challenge in coaching leaders is earning your seat at the executive table. Worth has a number of dimensions:

- **Worth for the leader (worth = value).** The leader knows their own situation best as it relates to their business, their background, their team, and the organization. So in the back of the coach's mind is the question: Do I understand the leader's challenges well enough to add value (i.e. worth) for them?

- **Content worth (worth = value).** Do I have the right content and resources to help them with their challenges?

- **Coach worth (value for the coach).** How can I spend more time in coaching sessions with leaders and less time in session preparation, admin, and follow-up? In the end, the value for the coach and the leader is in the face-to-face time, i.e. billable hours, and not in all the hours spent outside the coaching sessions. Do I have enough content to cover the entire coaching journey with the leader, lasting up to 12 months?

- **Worth (value for the client, Triple Win).** How do I make a difference for the leader, their team, and the client organization, delivering the impact they need to have a good return on investment for the coaching service? And how do I measure that impact properly, independently, and objectively so that that value is real and incontestable?

It is important to have this worth embedded in your coaching services so that you feel confident and excited to deliver value to the client.

## COMBINE YOUR WORTH WITH AN APPROACH THAT WORKS FOR ANY LEADER AND TEAM WHO GENUINELY STRIVE TO GET BETTER TOGETHER

Like many coaches, I truly want to help leaders improve, so I wanted an approach that works across cultures, countries, industries, and organizational levels. I knew there was no silver bullet, but I understood that combining best practices must lead to an optimal and, hopefully, a best-in-class coaching approach.

The journey started with a phone call from a fellow coach from the USA, who talked me through his experience and pointed me to a few coaching approaches and certifications. True to my own mantra to learn from others, I embraced his advice, bought a ticket, and jumped at the first opportunity to get certified in behavioral leadership coaching. That was probably one of the best investments I ever made. After this great start, however, the journey became less fruitful.

I got a few more certifications over the next six months; they provided a lot of knowledge and insights but fell short of my expectations.

Over the years, my journey led me to identify three main elements that contribute to coaching success, and I have integrated them into our coaching approach.

**Aligning coaching with existing organizational best practices:** Clients are typically not familiar with coaching, but they connect our coaching activities to familiar approaches they use within their organizations, such as the management of product development, projects, customer satisfaction, and even safety and the supply chain. Synthesizing these practices with coaching not only validates our approach but also encourages leaders to embrace change more readily.

**Achieving a cohesive, integrated coaching approach:** Numerous coaching certifications offer profound insights into human psychology and behavior that foster awareness for both the client and the coach. These various approaches need to be brought together as an integrated coaching service that meets the customer's needs and improves team effectiveness and performance results simultaneously.

**Incorporating readily applicable tools and resources:** While coaching certifications provide valuable knowledge, many lack ready-made tools and resources to apply in coaching engagements immediately. An optimal coaching approach should include a well-defined service proposition, mapped out over a 6 to 12-month timeframe, which yields measurable results.

By embracing these three elements, I worked to create a comprehensive and practical coaching approach that would build on the best practices already in use within organizations, allowing both leaders and teams to genuinely grow and improve together.

It took a lot of road-testing with clients. Over time, it grew into a consistent, predefined service proposition that fit with every coaching engagement I had—across multiple countries and industries, and with leaders at different levels, provided they want to create change together.

Most of the clients we work with are large multinationals. Having worked in such organizations myself for many years, a few things were already clear more than 15 years ago:

1. **Improve service quality and efficiency.** Over the last 50+ years, organizations have been focusing more and more on processification to improve quality and efficiency in everything they do. Starting in finance and manufacturing in the last century, the trend has moved into supply chain management, product development, and HR over the last few decades. Learning and development are the last frontiers for processification in the organization, with the trend taking hold in coaching and leadership development.

2. **Measurable results and return on investment.** Organizations do not just want to have value for money in a subjective sense. They want a clear return on investment that is demonstrated by facts and figures throughout the service delivery process. Decision-makers in organizations ask themselves, 'Is coaching worth it?'

In my professional career in large multinational organizations and process engineering, I have always been confronted with the question of return on investment. Is it worth it? Organizations dislike investing in things that don't have the right return on investment. In the early days of supply chain optimization, this discussion took the form of categorizing some of the benefits of the supply chain automation changes into qualitative and quantitative benefits. Quantitative benefits were considered to be objective, whereas qualitative benefits were considered to be subjective and something of a bonus. If the quantitative benefits of a decision looked reasonable in terms of return on investment, then it was a good idea, because the qualitative benefits would provide extra value down the road.

3. **Leading is cocreating change with coworkers.** In the USA and Japan, companies experimented very early on with leaders involving coworkers in change to improve organizational processes, approaches to work, products, and more. This structured involvement of coworkers was the foundation of many things we now take for granted, like quality circles, customer focus groups for product improvement, accountability practices in safety management, and upward feedback to management on what's happening in the organization. Even in microfinance, accountability groups were proven to be very successful.

# FOUR PILLARS OF LONG-TERM SUCCESS

To be successful in the coaching business in the long run, I knew that four things were really important:

- Being able to **measure results** and demonstrate the benefits of coaching to the organization using metrics familiar to them, such as increased revenue, faster execution, higher engagement of employees, and succession-readiness of managers.

- Creating a **structured service proposition** that can be delivered in an effective and efficient manner and is also **replicable** and **scalable**.

- **Applying technology** in service delivery where relevant; technology can deliver parts of the service **more efficiently** and even with **higher quality** than when managed by coaches themselves.

- **Involving coworkers** to provide suggestions and implement improvements and making these same coworkers collaborators in the change process. They need to be able to hold each other accountable, to cocreate change very much in the same way as they collaborate on other projects in their organizations.

Although it was not all that clear to me initially, these pillars of long-term success were brought into the coaching engagements early on. I was blessed to have great clients and teachers at the beginning. One of the first leaders I coached, Pauline, was the CEO of an FMCG company who had to manage a number of very challenging and seemingly contradictory objectives: reorganize the company, close factories and reduce cost, increase revenue, and engage employees— all within 12 months. Having just started out, I had my doubts about how to complete the engagement for the client successfully. However, Pauline was clear about the company's strategic vision and organized in her execution; she engaged her management team and made them part of the leadership change process. She was determined to fully apply this approach and cocreate change in collaboration with coworkers. Because everybody engaged in the process, we had results very early on.

In times of change, there is often no structure to rely on—for the basic reason that old structures are not working, which is *why* change is necessary in the first place. Being able to offer the client a structure to help them in the change process is something they embrace, and at the same time, it is very helpful for you as a coach.

Some of the first leaders I coached were very open about their leadership change to the people in their environment. They made it about the change that had to happen in the larger environment. Not only did they take their coworkers on the journey, they were also very strong in measuring impact. As CEO of an FMCG organization, Pauline was obsessed with measuring customer satisfaction. Consequently, she loved the idea of measuring the satisfaction of coworkers with leadership change. The Chief Financial Officer (CFO) made a full analysis of investment in the coaching impact on the leader, the team, and the business. The great case study they wrote demonstrated that the return on investment was 10,000% and the payback time was within six weeks. (Best practice industry standards regarding actual return on investment may be 25–100%, resulting in a payback time of one to four years.) You can see how this impact got a lot of people excited in the organization. As a result, they decided that I should coach other people in the management team as well to accelerate the change they were making. With a six-week payback time, that was just a no-brainer. With the training budget exhausted for other purposes already, the CEO redirected resources from consulting towards the coaching effort. Needless to say, this was a great success for the client and a great confidence-booster for me as a coach.

This experience, along with those with other early clients, confirmed three things for me:

- More structure creates more freedom to do more things.

- Measuring impact at the level of the leader, their team, and the organization keeps everybody focused, engaged, and accountable in the process.

- It's the client who determines the success of the leadership coaching engagement at the start. Everybody can change, but they have to want to.

## WORK WITH LEADERS WHO WANT TO CHANGE

These realizations led me to think about how to determine these success factors right from the get-go. Because there was a clear correlation between picking the right leader and using the right approach to get the right results, it was a causal relationship. With a good understanding of the right approach, it became really important to articulate what the right leader looks like.

For that, I looked at other behavioral change methodologies out there. I quickly found a lot of relevant analogies in behavioral change programs around habits. These ranged from quitting addictions (smoking, drugs, gambling, and eating) to improving habits to increase sports performance. And a few personality traits became obvious. It is not one habit functioning in isolation that needs to change. Good or bad habits are formed by other habits. If I want to change a cycle of behaviors, I can drive that change by leveraging habits I want to keep.

The three mindsets that drive that change are 'I go,' 'we go,' and 'let's go'. Leaders need to recognize that they are the center of the change and that it starts with them. They need to recognize and embrace that they can get better and that they need to be vulnerable and experiment with change. It's something they already do in their organizations when managing change in services or products. Leaders need to recognize that the people around them are aware of the changes that need to be made and are willing to support the change process because they will also benefit from it. Therefore, the leader needs to go the distance with their coworkers. Last but not least, it is simple to start a long journey, but it is not easy to finish a long journey. That is where follow-up, execution, and discipline come into play. The more I explored these personality traits at the start of the coaching journey, the clearer it became that success is determined at the outset. This further confirmed that the right client and the right coaching approach do create the right results.

# GET MEASURABLE SUCCESS
# 95% OF THE TIME

If you could wave a magic wand that ensures that 95% of your coaching engagements would be a raving success, as determined by the leader that you're coaching, their manager, and their coworkers, would you sign up for that as a coach? I bet you would. In this book, I am going to explain how to do exactly that. What I'm going to share with you in this book has been road-tested with more than a million leaders and has been shown to ensure a 95% success rate of getting better in the eyes of their coworkers. And 98% of the leaders enjoyed their change journey, even to the extent that I as a coach can guarantee 100% that leaders get results.

# ELEARNING RESOURCES

Chapter resources and demos are available in your eLearning account. Sign up and access it here: www.globalcoachgroup.com/triplewinbook or email coach@globalcoachgroup.com

# CHAPTER 3

# LIGHT UP YOUR LEADERSHIP COACHING SUCCESS

Success as a leadership coach means helping clients get better for themselves and their teams

As coaches, we want to be a guiding light. The challenges we face are best expressed in the words of Marianne Williamson:

> Our deepest fear is not that we are inadequate. Our deepest fear is that we are powerful beyond measure. It is our light, not our darkness, that most frightens us. We ask ourselves, 'Who am I to be brilliant, gorgeous, talented, fabulous?' Actually, who are you not to be? You are a child of God. You're playing small, which does not serve the world. There is nothing enlightened about shrinking so that other people won't feel insecure around you. We are all meant to shine, as children do. We were born to manifest the glory of God that is within us. It's not just in some of us; it's in everyone. And as we let our own light shine, we unconsciously give other people permission to do the same. As we are liberated from our own fear, our presence automatically liberates others.

## TURNING YOUR CANDLELIGHT INTO A SPOTLIGHT TO GUIDE YOUR JOURNEY

I first read this quote in Williamson's book *A Return to Love* and saw it again in the movie *Coach Carter* in 2005. These profound words have guided my journey as a corporate leader and later as a leadership coach throughout the years. They have inspired me to train thousands of coaches worldwide and led me to explore the fundamental questions that coaches often grapple with in their journey to success.

By the end of this chapter, you will know how to embrace that guiding light, the keys to success to light up the path of the leaders you are coaching, and what you can do to bring this into your coaching practice.

What turned my candlelight into a spotlight was a compelling desire to make a difference, and the spark that truly excited me was the staggering reality revealed by numerous engagement studies that less than one-third of employees were engaged at work. A pivotal key to transforming this engagement, I discovered, rested in the hands of one person—the leader, as the manager of their team. This revelation drove my passion to help leaders become better.

Coaching a leader was a promising start, as it is relatively easy to inspire and guide them towards self-improvement, which is a significant victory in itself. The ultimate goal, however, is to ensure that their entire team becomes, and remains, highly engaged. Most coaching engagements are sponsored by client organizations, and these leaders' managers eagerly await tangible evidence of improvements.

After an intensive coaching engagement, the real challenge emerges: sitting down with the leader's manager to review the journey. The leader customarily sings the praises of the coaching service, thrilled by the transformation it has sparked in them. However, the manager has their own perspective, built on their observations and on feedback from those working closely with the leader. Discussions can be marked by differing opinions, leaving doubts about whether the leader had indeed improved measurably in the eyes of the manager and others and, thus, whether the coaching investment was justified.

This is where involving coworkers in the coaching process flips the script. With my background in data-driven organizational management, I was uncomfortable relying solely on the coach's and leader's opinions as evidence of improvement. Both had vested interests in claiming success, and there were no data points from others in the organization to validate progress.

By actively engaging managers from the start and regularly collecting the opinions of coworkers, we created a robust system of cocreation and accountability. The coach, leader, and manager all had a stake in ensuring the leader was perceived as improving in the eyes of their coworkers. This change made the coaching smoother, and it was no longer about convincing others but rather about celebrating achievements.

Including coworkers and measuring their satisfaction yielded remarkable results. Leaders improved more readily, managers recognized the change in the leader and their teams, and these coworkers actively participated in aiding their leader's growth. The whole approach started working seamlessly, like a well-oiled machine.

Early on in my coaching journey, CEOs and CFOs would all hit me with the same question before and during the coaching engagements: 'What is the ROI (return on investment)?' All the calculations they made regarding coaching for their managers consistently showed returns ranging from 1,000% to over 10,000%. The coaching benefits extended not only to the leaders but also to their coworkers. This realization of a 10–100X ROI became a defining pinnacle, highlighting why coaching works.

- First, a 10–100X return on investment outperforms most other corporate investments and ensures a payback time of a few months.

- Second, clients witnessing their results changed the energy around the coaching service. Even CFOs get excited about coaching, proclaiming it as the company's best investment in years. This is truly exceptional and not just satisfying for me as a coach.

- More importantly, when coaching is seen as a highly profitable solution to organizational challenges, the whole concept takes wings and becomes a eureka moment for the decision-making executives.

This journey taught me that coaching could lead to profound and measurable change, benefiting not only individual leaders but also their teams and their performance results. It was transforming leaders, engaging teams, and even winning over the most skeptical managerial or financial minds—a most worthwhile endeavor for all.

## YOUR BRILLIANCE IS YOUR LIGHT

Now, I'm turning this back to you with a question: 'What is the light in you that the world is waiting for?' That question has echoed in the minds of countless coaches. As a coach, you possess unique brilliance, talent, and perspective. However, it's common for self-doubt to creep in, leading you to question whether you are worthy of shining your light.

The truth is, you are more powerful and capable than you might believe. We are all born with the potential to make a significant impact in this world. Playing small does not serve anyone. It's time to step into your greatness because, as Marianne Williamson beautifully puts it, 'As we let our own light shine, we unconsciously give other people permission to do the same.'

Reflecting on my earlier story, what truly benefitted me was the realization that I didn't have to constantly justify the effectiveness of my approach to the leader's manager or others within the client organization. Quite the opposite. The coaching light I shed on the leader's path, guiding them to become a more effective leader for their team and achieve better results, received applause and recognition from their managers and team members. This added fuel to the fire in an incredibly positive way. I gained precisely what I know you can derive from this too: You will be able to replicate my success, just as thousands of coaches have done using the methodology I've shared with them over the years.

## BRIGHTENING THE JOURNEY

To make your light shine bright and make it all worthwhile, coaches need to address a few key challenges, which I have briefly outlined below. These major points will be unpacked further over the course of the book.

# 1. Customization and structure is a balancing act

One common misconception among coaches is that structure and customization are mutually exclusive. This couldn't be further from the truth. In fact, structure provides the freedom and opportunities needed to create a customized approach that leads to success. A structured yet agile framework empowers you to tailor your coaching services to each client's unique needs while maintaining a consistent, robust, and effective approach.

# 2. Identifying the real client

In the realm of leadership coaching, it's essential to identify who the real client is. Is it the individual being coached, the team members they lead, or the manager who is sponsoring the coaching engagement? Again, organizations invest in coaching with the expectation of a return on their investment. While leaders might feel satisfied with their coaching experience, the impact on their teams and coworkers can be less significant. However, both of these aspects are crucially important to the manager investing in the coaching (on behalf of the organization).

# 3. Measuring the impact of coaching

Another prevalent misconception is that measuring the impact of coaching and leadership change is difficult. On the contrary, the more engaged team members are in the leadership process, the easier and quicker you can achieve remarkable results and measure their impact.

Coaches must understand that leadership is a team sport, and it's in the perception of the team members that leadership transformation truly happens. As team members become more actively involved in the leadership change process, measuring the impact through their perceptions and the resulting performance improvements becomes more accurate and tangible.

## 4. Overcoming internal doubts

All of the above points cause many coaches to grapple with internal doubts. Such doubts revolve around three key areas: the adequacy of their know-how, the relevance and meaningfulness of their service, and the results they can deliver to clients. It's crucial for coaches to recognize their unique expertise and the value they bring to their clients.

# THE TRIPLE WIN FOR THE LEADER

Clients want meaningful value from their coaching service. How about this? Would this work for you? Imagine having a coaching service tailored to each client, delivered efficiently, and with a 95% success rate of the coworkers confirming the improvements made by the leader, their team, and the organizational performance. What would these measurable results mean for you as a coach and your coaching service? Would it significantly enhance your value and the services you offer? If your answer is yes, then this book is for you.

Addressing the above challenges has been the focus of my journey and has resulted in a coaching methodology that delivers the

Triple Win, which forms the foundation of the Triple Win Coaching approach.

Drawing from my professional experiences, I have incorporated renowned service success factors and fused them with valuable insights. This combination serves as a potent reminder that coaching success hinges on a delicate interplay of various factors, such as credibility, reliability, customer intimacy, and the absence of self-interest. These elements not only bolster trustworthiness but also act as critical determinants of a coach's efficacy based on their particular background.

In the end, leadership coaching is not about just one individual but about cocreating change with coworkers. A trusted coaching approach plays a vital role in each engagement.

## THE FIVE BIG STEPS

Throughout this book, we'll follow a roadmap for coaching success. If I were to condense this into five significant steps, it would be these:

1. **Start Smart and Set Yourself Up for Success:** Begin your coaching journey by defining clear goals and expectations for yourself and your clients.

2. **Focus on the Few Areas that Matter:** Identify the most critical areas of development for your clients, ensuring that your coaching efforts are impactful.

3. **Cocreation:** Recognize that change is a collective effort, and involving others in the process can make it more meaningful.

4. **Structure:** Implementing a structured approach simplifies the coaching service, making it easier to achieve desired outcomes.

5. **Overcome Challenges and Measure Results:** Understand that challenges are part of the journey, and measuring results is essential for tracking progress.

# NO RISK, ALL REWARD

As a coach embarking on this journey with the help of this book, you'll be equipped to attain your own Triple Win of more impact, more coaching, and more clients. Here's what to expect:

1. **More Impact:** By unleashing your full potential as a coach, this book empowers you with insights, tools, and resources to create lasting and meaningful change for your clients, making a genuine difference in their lives and the lives of their coworkers.

2. **More Coaching:** Developing a transparent service grounded in proven principles that consistently deliver measurable results enhances your credibility and fosters trust in your abilities.

3. **More Clients:** By focusing on the outcomes that truly matter to clients, you position yourself as a true partner in their success, free from conflicts of interest.

This book is your roadmap to thrive as a coach, as I share proven strategies and structures that have produced results. Drawing upon the experiences of one million leaders worldwide and their teams, we will break down these concepts step by step, guiding you toward delivering tangible results and unlocking your coaching potential.

Are you prepared to embark on this transformative journey and become a truly impactful leadership coach? The answers await us as we set forth on the path to mobilize your full potential.

# ELEARNING RESOURCES

Chapter resources and demos are available in your eLearning account. Sign up and access it here: www.globalcoachgroup.com/triplewinbook or email coach@globalcoachgroup.com

CHAPTER 4

# START SMART

Success for you and your client
starts immediately

They say, 'If you sell well, then all the *what-ifs* in the coaching journey take care of themselves.' All too often, my discussions with coaches center on this question: 'What if my client changes their mind around their commitment to coaching during the engagement?', or 'What if the manager does not genuinely support the leader in the coaching engagement?' I've heard about a hundred different 'what if' scenarios from coaches over my many years in the business. They're all plausible, and they can all be resolved by aligning the key decision-makers in the *sales* process of the coaching engagement. Yes, that early.

If you sell well, then most of the *what-ifs* will be taken care of at the outset, proactively, and the coaching journey becomes a smooth ride for you and the leader. If you don't sell well, you'll stumble throughout the coaching journey and need to resolve challenges as they occur reactively, and the coaching journey might feel like an uphill battle.

By the end of this chapter, you'll know exactly how to set your clients up for success right from the start, which adds big time to your success as a coach in each engagement. Everything I'm sharing with you is based on training, mentoring, and working with more than 4,000 coaches worldwide who are part of our Global Coach Group network. And these coaches, including myself, have in turn coached countless leaders around the world. I alone have coached for more than 20,000 hours, and after all that experience, I can tell you this: Starting smart is your key to success. I will share with you how to do just that.

# GET BUY-IN FROM DECISION-MAKERS

The first step in 'starting smart' is to align all the decision-makers around the coaching service proposition. We all know the proverb 'No pain, no gain.' In coaching, the contrary is true. If you start smart, you can organize the coaching journey for gain without pain, for you and the leader alike.

The choice is simple. As a coach, do you have the courage and craft to manage the *what-ifs* at the start of the coaching engagement and set yourself up for success? Or will you choose to let them be and hope that they evaporate over time, or manage them down the road in the coaching engagement?

Sometimes, the *what-ifs* are very clear upfront and staring you in the face. In other cases, they are disguised in the initial conversations and can become real pitfalls down the road if not managed well upfront. It's the more subtle and hidden *what-if* scenarios that you need to keep an eye out for and manage well upfront. Here are some of the common *what-ifs* and how to manage them.

## What if the manager doesn't really want the coaching for their team?

Early on in my coaching career, I was asked by a CEO to coach one of his direct reports, who was destined to be the CEO's successor within 18 months. I was very excited about that engagement as a great marker of coaching success for a number of reasons:

1. This was actually a major promotion for this leader, who was to become the first head of function to replace an expatriate in that position throughout the organization.

2. It was a great chance to demonstrate the efficacy of coaching, not only for leaders to improve but also for making people ready to step up to the next level in their professional careers (succession-readiness).

3. I knew the CEO on a personal and professional level—at least, I thought I did—so this looked to be an easy ride.

4. Last but not least, it would be my first time coaching such a high-level leader, one whose next stop was the top-level position in their organization.

I thought this very visible coaching engagement would be a game-changer for me. Why? Well, I knew the manager and the leader quite well, as I had worked with the organization as a coach and leadership development consultant before, and it felt like everyone involved was committed to the coaching process. Surely a coaching journey starting with a manager excited about investing in a leader willing to participate would be successful. I envisioned how many amazing blessings I could bring to the engagement for this leader and the organization.

As these things typically go, the coaching engagement started with a lot of excitement by all involved—the CEO, the head of HR, and of course, the leader. The initial feedback assessments included a lot of valuable information, and my only concern was that the leader might be hesitant to select the right areas to develop. That concern quickly evaporated in the feedback debriefing session: The challenges the leader chose were *being more disciplined in execution* and *being more decisive*. I knew these were exactly the areas the manager had in mind, and that they had been voiced by other coworkers as well.

The initial coaching sessions went very well. I coached the leader on making great action plans that were articulate and specific. The leader had a knack for doing things to perfection and was very resilient and exemplary in working hard. I felt that everything was pretty much going in the right direction.

When it came time for the quarterly leadership pulse review, opinions on how the leader was developing were collected from the various coworkers. The leader's manager was surprisingly negative. The head of HR was reluctant to provide their input, as they claimed they hadn't interacted enough with the leader to provide a clear opinion. The opinions of other coworkers were quite positive, as I had expected. As a result, the coaching engagement that started so well with great fanfare came to a grinding halt after six months. It was stopped by the manager.

The leader was upset about the situation, and I was puzzled about what happened to make the engagement go pear-shaped. By contrast, the manager didn't seem to care much. This was clearly not the success I had envisioned from the initial discussions with the CEO, HR, and the leader. I didn't find out what had been going on behind the scenes until a few months later, while I was working with another CEO in the region. As it turns out, the CEO had never been quite invested in the coaching of his direct report, hoping instead that the coaching would demonstrate that the leader should not be promoted to be their successor—because the CEO didn't want to move away from his position in the first place.

Reviewing the situation, I realized that I should not have assumed that, by default, the CEO would be supportive of the whole coaching process (even though he had given all the lip service that was expected early on). With the coaching engagement cut short, I missed out on a substantial part of the contracted coaching fees, which was a very expensive lesson 'to not assume but confirm'—at least with a tacit agreement. I hadn't applied the rules in Start Smart (Chapter 4) that I knew were required.

Having the courage to get clarity up front pays great dividends for the client and the coach along the way. So, I started to use these specific questions at the beginning of each coaching engagement to align the key decision-makers.

1. Are you willing to support your leader and spend 5–10 minutes a month giving them a few suggestions on how they can improve?

2. Are you willing to support your leader and spend 5–10 minutes every quarter to assess with an open mind the progress the leader has made since the start of the coaching engagement?

3. How is this leader perceived in your organization? Are they a high performer, about average, or in the low performers' group?

What you need at the beginning is clarity, not executive poetry. These three questions are deliberately articulated to get short and clear answers to which you can hold the decision-makers accountable later on as necessary—in case, for example, the manager needs a nudge to step up and support a leader in their development journey if the engagement gets into troubled waters. Weave these questions into the conversation with decision-makers during the sales process, and they will come across as very conversational and natural.

Here's a tip: After your introduction discussion with that manager, send them a nice thank-you email that also confirms that you have had this 3-question discussion and they are willing to support team members. You can even emphasize in this email how amazing they are and how their leader is blessed with such a supportive manager on their side.

You can use the same line of questioning with other key decision-makers, like the Chief Human Resources Officer (CHRO), if they are involved.

Not long after this experience, I got an even bigger and better engagement. Having learned my lessons, before I committed myself to the engagement, I tried to ensure there was alignment between the leader to be coached and the decision-makers (the global CEO as their manager and the head of HR). Here's what happened.

## What if the leader doesn't want the coaching?

The global CEO of a large consumer goods organization called me to coach a typical high-performing and hard-driving regional CEO, Bob. The engagement was very straightforward. 'Will, please coach Bob. I believe in coaching, I know that you can do it, you have all my support, and it doesn't matter what the fees are because the return on investment is clear.' He went on to say, 'I want Bob to be successful as regional CEO, and at this moment, he is on the road to destruction. I know your coaching method is the one we really need, and I know that you as his coach could really pull this off. But I really want to see results. Otherwise, these coaching engagements have little future in our organization.' That was music to my ears, as I am sure you understand. A dream coaching engagement.

Based on lessons learned, I made sure to lock in the manager's commitment right from the start—explicitly. I could tell this global CEO was totally on board. He gloriously passed my 3-question test and was very explicit about doing everything necessary to make this work. The head of HR was fully involved in the process and went along with everything in a very committed manner. So, all the boxes were ticked.

The next challenge was to talk to the leader in question and see how he looked at the coaching journey and what his level of commitment would be. I very vividly remember that I was in a hotel in Dubai right on the beach when I had that 30-minute phone conversation with Bob. In typical executive style, Bob was very positive about his manager, their business, and himself. He politely enquired about the coaching journey and how it would unfold. I was warned by his manager that Bob was both very articulate and very good at being in denial about the real issues. Having learned that being specific about starting smart really helps in the coaching journey, I asked questions about his commitment to it. Bob was very positive and affirmative; we were on the right footing from the very beginning. The commitments that he made as a leader really helped in every session thereafter. On more occasions than one, this served me well with Bob. For example, at one point, he wanted to exclude certain key executive team members as coworkers from the coaching. Since we had discussed this in our initial meeting and confirmed thereafter, I could easily bring him back to this in our conversations and hold him accountable. This sort of thing doesn't have to be very heavy, by the way. It can be as simple as, 'Remember our initial meeting, when we discussed that involving coworkers in the coaching program is very effective and pivotal to your success, as it increases your success rate from 18% to 95%?' This particular leader was actually a very high-ego personality. When people with big egos make commitments, they tend to stand by them.

## For the leader, I use these three questions

'To take your leadership to the next level, are you willing to:

- Commit to a 12-month journey to improve as a leader and move to the next level in your performance?

- Invest five minutes a day in reviewing your action plan?

- Involve your team members and manager in this journey, and ask them for suggestions to improve and work to get better together?'

These questions are very simple and straightforward, and they get easy yes answers from leaders without conditions or provisions. Again, this helps you to refer back to that conversation down the road in the engagement if need be. I will expand on why these questions are articulated in this way when we talk about the structure of the coaching service and engagement in the following chapters. Then you will see how impactful and amazing they really are.

Remember, when a coach is being hired, this information is not visible unless they *ask these questions*. Don't jump into the coaching in good faith without having a clear picture of what is really going on behind the scenes. Such coaching engagements might look very crisp, clean, and supportive, but a couple of months down the road, you might begin to discover how many intricate issues were in the background all along. This makes the journey very challenging, even frustrating, for the leader—and for the coach too, as all their help and support falls on deaf ears. Beyond frustration, the experience can result in a strong negative impact on your brand and reputation as a coach.

In hindsight, it was good to go through these tests and trials to find the right methods to apply in coaching. But I can tell you it took a lot of time, effort, and pain to put it all in place. And pain it honestly was. In coaching engagements where the leader is operating in an unsupported environment (and it doesn't matter whether it is their fault or the fault of the organization), there can be a lot of drama and pain, leading to disengagement and even people leaving the organization. This is very, very sad for the leaders themselves, and it negatively affects their team and the people they are working with. As a coach, you are trying to do great work by helping leaders become better and more effective with their team; you don't want it ending up in a 'car wreck' and with unpaid bills.

Since I have been using these coaching questions in the sales process, there have been zero cases where the wrong leaders started coaching without the support of their manager, and none that were canceled prematurely because people were exited from the organization.

# DETERMINE COACHABILITY
# TO START SMART

## Select the right clients who want to go the distance

This sounds obvious and simple, but often it is not. If you try to coach the wrong client, the coaching engagement can easily become an uphill battle with little or no results down the road. This is not helpful for anybody. Trust me, I have tried it more than once, and each time I realized that I should have followed my own advice.

As coaches, there are times when we see people we know can benefit from our services. We go after them because we genuinely want to help them be better in their personal life and at work. And though that logic sounds commendable, it is actually the wrong logic. Not everybody with a problem wants to invest in resolving that problem or wants to be helped by a coach. I was blessed to learn this lesson early on in my coaching career when I did some work with Stephen Covey and others in his team. Repeatedly in our conversations, the idea arose that a coach can only help people who want to be helped. That is the lens to use in selecting your clients.

This isn't as easy as just taking people's word for it that they really want to do something about the challenges that they're facing. You need to peel back more of the layers, get to the essence of what their challenges are, and whether they are committed to going the distance to work towards the solution they want to embrace. This shouldn't be surprising. Many people want to be more fit and healthy, but not all of them are willing to set aside the food they crave and exercise and sweat to bring their fitness and health goals into reality.

Selecting the right client is not about the type of personality you're dealing with. It is really about recognizing the challenges in the coaching engagement that could be *what-ifs* down the road. Again, they need to be addressed upfront to understand whether the client is willing to commit to overcoming these hurdles. Though *what-if* challenges appear in many forms, many of them can be boiled down to these core issues coaches face during engagements:

- **Losing momentum and the coaching engagement fizzles out**

   Like New Year's resolutions, coaching engagements start with a lot of excitement and momentum. At the start of the coaching journey, many newly discovered awareness lightbulbs begin switching on for the client as various assessments and feedback sessions give new insights to the leader. That is great news for smart people—which most leaders are—as it tickles their intellect. However, the real hard work comes later on in the coaching engagement, when the leader needs to focus on the grinding work towards results. This part is more about brawn than brain, much less exciting but necessary. Just like our New Year's resolution to get fitter, the grinding work is down the road when we have to keep going to the gym to do the same exercise routine again and again to sweat our way to success.

- **The action plan does not include the right solutions**

   Without a doubt, put a leader and a coach together and you get a powerful combination of leadership experience and intellect that can be trusted to create sophisticated action plans. But that's no guarantee that the solutions they crafted together will be effective in the leader's work environment.

Let me give you an actual example, which also comes from early on in my coaching career. I had been working with Alex, the country CEO of an automotive company, for a number of months to improve her ability to be more effective in decision-making. The various coaching sessions had been very insightful for Alex, and I had brought in some high-quality resources from Harvard and IMD business schools for the leader to improve in this particular area. And Alex, being super-smart, had made some very impressive action plans. With her endless energy, she didn't lack the commitment to be consistent and persistent in her execution. Yet after a couple of months, we did a check-in on the leader's progress, and the results were not as good as we had expected. Why? I did some further digging into the results, and it turned out that Alex had left out a major ingredient in the whole process.

Several of Alex's coworkers voiced that the decision-making meetings with her were long. This was because many people in the executive team shared their opinions, and there were often long-lasting debates about the ways to address the problems facing the business. In the end, people agreed that although Alex was excited about the decisions made, she didn't really integrate the opinions of other executives into the ultimate solutions. A key ingredient to effective decision-making is 'listening to other people's opinions' and 'integrating other people's opinions into the ultimate solution'. These two actions were absent from the action plan altogether.

## Client coachability factors

Over the years, I have learned that the right clients are those willing to commit to three coachability factors:

- **Right Focus:** Are they willing to focus their leadership development on the issues that matter as much to their coworkers as they matter to them?

- **Cocreation:** Are they willing to involve their coworkers and collaborate with them on leadership change and cocreate results together?

- **Discomfort:** Change is about doing things in different ways, which by definition makes people uncomfortable. The question is: Are they willing to work through this discomfort and find new ways to succeed?

One way to make your assessment is to ask questions during the initial conversation focusing on these three coachability factors. Integrating these questions into your conversation with prospective clients will help you gauge their readiness for coaching and set the stage for successful outcomes. Getting the right clients immediately ensures a strong and productive relationship focusing on continuous growth and improvement.

**Here is a list of questions to assess the three coachability factors:**

1. *Right Focus Questions:*

    1.1. Can you identify specific leadership or team challenges that currently impact both you and your coworkers?

    1.2. Are you open to selecting improvement areas that matter to your coworkers as much as they matter to you?

1.3. If you significantly improve the challenges you mentioned earlier, how would it impact your effectiveness and that of your team? In other words, what difference will it make, and does it matter?

2. *Cocreation Questions:*

2.1. In many of your business processes, you involve coworkers to cocreate change, as this brings better ideas and better results faster. Are you willing to use a similar approach and leverage their insights and suggestions to improve both your own and your team's effectiveness?

2.2. Considering why you involve coworkers in other business processes, what would be the value of involving them in improving team and leadership effectiveness?

2.3. How will sustained leadership effectiveness change impact your team's culture, engagement, and effectiveness?

3. *Discomfort Questions:*

3.1. When you get constructive feedback and suggestions from others, how does that make you feel?

3.2. Change requires trying new ways of doing things that are likely to cause discomfort at times. What is your way of working through this?

3.3. How disciplined are you to work through the challenges and go the distance to attain the results you are looking for, both for you and your team? Is it worth it for us to go the distance together?

To gain a deeper understanding of these coachability factors and how to use them effectively in your coaching conversations, you can access a video in the eLearning resources provided at the end of this chapter. The video offers practical examples and guidance on integrating these questions seamlessly into your client interactions and maximizing their impact on coaching outcomes.

## Putting the three coachability factors to work

The more you keep the three coachability factors (right focus, cocreation and discomfort) in the forefront of your mind when you talk to new clients, the easier it will be to recognize and select the right ones. A few years back, I was interviewing a top global executive at a Fortune 100 company in the USA, and early in our discussion, Adam casually mentioned that he was an avid marathon runner. I immediately steered the discussion deeper into his marathon passion to understand his approach to goal-setting, selecting the right focus for improvement, working on incremental change with micro-behaviors, the discipline around implementing training plans, and dealing with challenges and discomfort along the way. Not surprisingly, he came up with all the right answers. I used his marathon passion as a stand-in to explain the coaching journey and how the three coachability factors are critical to success. Needless to say, he immediately understood what was required for success throughout the coaching journey; at the same time, it confirmed for him that our working together was a great fit.

Understanding and recognizing these coachability factors comes in handy in the initial client conversations. It helps you to keep an eye out for what is really important in the coaching journey, to find usable examples and analogies in what the client is saying, and to steer the conversation. Most importantly, you won't need to convince the client about anything because they will already have convinced themselves that these are important factors for success. The only thing you need to do is use their examples to illustrate how they apply in the leadership coaching journey. This sets you and the client up for success from the start, distinguishing you from the various coaches the client interviews.

Sometimes, the main challenge is in the coach's head. They know that they can help the leader because they have all the necessary tools and experience and can envision the right solutions. However, the leader doesn't necessarily have that same level of conviction, or their manager (or other decision-makers) is not fully supportive. Trying to convince the leader or their manager is a very noble undertaking, but it can turn into an uphill battle.

As a coach, you should consider what your most valuable asset is. Is it *impact* (i.e. helping leaders to be better), or is it *time*? Many coaches focus on helping leaders to make the impact they know is important and meaningful. The question you should ask is: How much time are you willing to invest to try to make this impact a reality for the leader? With committed leaders, you will reap more meaning for less time, but with less committed leaders, you will spend more time yet get less meaning. That is the main trade-off that coaches need to make. Selecting the right leaders is going to save you a lot of time and create a whole lot more meaning. This reaps the benefits for the leader, their manager, other decision-makers, and last but not least, their team. Everybody wins. This is the time/meaning trade-off. The best results I have achieved have been with leaders I have spent the *least* time with; the worst results have been with those I spent the *most* time with. The inverse correlation between more impact and less time helps me select the right clients and make even more impact. I am sure it will help you too.

I've prepared an eLearning resource for you to help you strengthen your skills in this area. Access links are at the end of this chapter.

When there is coachability and commitment between you and the client about the coaching service and the journey for the leader, and all these parameters have been agreed upon, then you have set yourself up for success. This is starting smart. Now it is time to begin the coaching journey with the leader, and that is going to be explained in the next chapter.

## ELEARNING RESOURCES

Chapter resources and demos are available in your eLearning account. Sign up and access it here: www.globalcoachgroup.com/triplewinbook or email coach@globalcoachgroup.com

CHAPTER 5

# A COMMITTED START

Commitment makes change
worthwhile – WHY

In my younger years, back in prep school, I studied classic languages and was inspired by many great Greek and Roman philosophers. One of Socrates' ideas has lingered in my mind and been very useful in coaching. He said that the secret to change hinges on two conditions. First, the desire to change must be greater than the desire to stay the same. Second, to change is to focus all of your energy not on fighting the old, but on building the new. In other words, individuals need strong motivation and a clear vision of an improved outcome before they commit to change and put in the necessary efforts.

When you create a coaching journey with more traction and less friction, momentum comes naturally. However, that might sound easier said than done. I'll show you three easy steps to create exactly that.

- Bring the future reality into the now.

- Help leaders course-correct their journey.

- Sacrifice a little time and effort now to ensure lasting benefits and rewards later.

The main issue in this chapter is the *Why*. Why should the leader invest time and effort in their coaching journey? What benefits do they get now, in the next months, and later on, past the coaching engagement?

Let's get a little more clarity around those three steps by thinking of them as principles:

1. **The Far View:** Articulating the destination of your journey to create a far view that is aspirational and empowering and has a lot of value for your client, and how to use that far-view value in every coaching session.

2. **Momentum Now:** Creating a safe setting for the leader to be energized and start with great momentum on the journey. This is also about creating a safe setting to involve coworkers in the coaching journey, which can provide a lot of immediate momentum.

3. **Agile Change with Low Effort:** Leaders are time-starved and at the same time, very smart. You want to create an environment where the leader doesn't need to do a lot of learning and doesn't need to be spending a lot of time. So, a little time, a little effort, and a little learning to create agile change. Sacrificing a little time and effort now ensures many lasting benefits and rewards later.

Most coaching programs start with a lot of energy and excitement around the newness of the coaching for the leader. Typically, they appreciate the attention and the privilege, and many lightbulbs go off. This sparks more awareness and deeper insights. Again, most leaders are very smart, and all this intellectual stimulus is what they love and embrace.

But new ideas and insights don't mean new behaviors and habits, and surely don't equate to any positive results for impact yet. All that hard work is still to come. Many people don't want to put in much effort to get to that 'new you'. They don't want to invest their energy as sweat equity (putting in effort rather than money as a way to create value) to get the benefits that the 'new you' can provide.

After the initial excitement and enlightenment, the energy levels drop: This is the time when real efforts are required to implement change—and when results don't come as quickly as leaders expect. Then they find it hard to keep the momentum going. In this phase, the coaching process is in danger of fizzling out over time for various reasons (not unlike diet and fitness programs). As a coach, you want to have several tools to keep the momentum going and improve the speed of change as the leader encounters challenges and obstacles.

# WHY – START WITH WHY AND DEFINE THE DESTINATION OF THE JOURNEY

Let's start with the first principle, articulating the far view. I recall a very powerful advertisement I saw many years ago, which still resonates with me today. The ad was about quitting smoking, and it asked, *'Which smile do you want your loved ones to see ten years from now?'* Below that, it featured two contrasting images: one of a person with severely decayed teeth, and the other of the same person with a radiant smile, a full set of beautiful teeth, and a warm, welcoming face.

Underneath these images, the copy simply stated, *'The choices you make daily will determine the smile people will see later.'* The message was clear, direct, and incredibly impactful. As they say, 'A picture is worth a thousand words,' and this ad demonstrated that perfectly. Every time I recall this advertisement, the powerful imagery instantly comes to mind, and that same visual representation is what you'll see in the illustration below.

I thought that was a very powerful word picture. The advertisement really hit me and made it clear how simple all this can be. What we do in coaching is exactly that: We work with a leader to paint that far-view picture.

Let me show you how we do this with the real-life example of Sanjiv, an executive I have been coaching in the financial services industry.

ones to see ten years from now?

the smile people will see later.

## Chart the journey in four questions

1. **Will:** What are the one or two things that attracted you to your current role in this organization and that brought you to where you are today?

   **Sanjiv:** Well, money makes the world go around; it is the oxygen for our lives. I'm passionate about helping people manage their lives through financial services. Money is like fuel, nourishing the fire of our ambitions and aspirations. Step by step, our financial products, such as loans, mortgages, savings, and credit cards, empower individuals and businesses to reach their goals. In my current role, I'm taking charge of how we do that. I'm shaping the kind of people we help, how we help them, and how we measure our impact. It not only gives meaning and purpose to my work, but it also allows me to see the positive ripples we create in the lives of our customers and beyond. It's quite rewarding to be a catalyst for change and growth!

2. **Will:** Then, moving from here, imagine we fast-forward to the end of our 12-month coaching engagement. What do you want people to say?

**Sanjiv:** I want people to say that they see me as not only customer-centric but also employee-centric. The word 'care' is something we use a lot in our organization, and I want them to feel that care also applies to each person in our team. That reminds me of what one of my former managers told me often, and it's almost funny. Obviously, we do risk management related to our clients. And leadership is about helping our people to grow and develop to empower them. That is also about taking a risk on people. And one of the comments from my former manager that always plays back in my mind is: I know I came here because somebody took a risk on me.

So I want my team to feel that I am taking a risk on them, but I also have their back. I'm here to help them to succeed. I'm not here to evaluate their performance; I'm here to help them to succeed. If I help everyone succeed, then we all succeed. We are all in this together.

It's a challenge at times because we deal with a lot of challenges and problems. Of course, that's what work is all about and sometimes these debates are heated. I want people to feel that we do this, that we fight for the customer—and as we fight for the customer, we also support each other to succeed.

3. **Will:** We're still at the 12-month mark on celebration day. What are the benefits that you want to have gained from the leadership coaching journey?

   **Sanjiv:** The benefits I want to gain from this journey are to develop patience and persistence, akin to a sculptor crafting a masterpiece. In doing so, I will build a more composed and stress-free demeanor and will be better at seeing the big picture while prioritizing and sequencing our strategy implementation effectively and empowering people in the process. I also hope to enhance my executive presence, which will open doors for more influential interactions within the organization. Ultimately, this journey will lead me to achieve better work–life harmony, fostering both personal and professional relationships in a more profound and meaningful way.

4. **Will:** Then, on the back of that: When you step into the shoes of the people who work with you, notably your team, what benefits do you want them to get?

   **Sanjiv:** I want my team members to be part of my transformation, as what helps us will help them too and whatever changes I make need to fit their approach to work. It needs to be a more collective change, where I take the lead. They should feel supported in adopting a growth mindset and embracing new challenges. I envision a more collaborative and inclusive decision-making process, where everyone feels connected and engaged. Similar to how a hive of bees works in harmony, I want my team to flourish in the nurturing environment of shared knowledge, trust, and teamwork. In this vibrant ecosystem, I can see our team attracting new talent, deepening the bench strength, and developing a solid succession plan. Together, we can strive for excellence and create a lasting impact on our organization and on their professional career. Doing this well is worth it. Thank you for waking me up to that. That's really useful.

The answers to these questions capture that far view that the leader is aspiring to. You want to capture what has been said. I literally put these things on one piece of paper to get a great overview of what that leader is working towards. And it is going to articulate the why for them: Why are they doing this? That is the big prize, the pot of gold at the end of the rainbow.

## HOW 1 – SAFE ENVIRONMENT FOR SUCCESS = 'HOW TO' JOURNEY

Now the leader knows WHERE they're going and they know WHY they're going there. If you can provide them with a safe and easy way to get there (HOW), then you are set to achieve success together. Before we proceed with the conversation with Sanjiv, let's look at fostering safe environments.

There are various ways to create safe and easy ways for leaders to open up and invite their coworkers into the conversation. I want to share one with you. It is not the only way, but it has proven to be very successful in working with all types of leaders around the world. You can do this in a very conversational and easy manner with the leader and do it more or less together.

*Let me show you how to create that safe and easy way, based on my conversation with Sanjiv. It starts with a little intro.*

**Will:** Sanjiv, as we are partnering in your coaching journey, I want you to know that based on our coaching experience, success in leadership and leadership change requires leaders to be 'we-centered' in their leadership thinking and behavior rather than 'me-centered'. Let me explain, and then I will ask you what this means in your environment. We-centered leadership starts with 'I go'. Leaders have to initiate their change: They need to step into the change themselves and commit to doing what it takes, get out of their comfort zone, and be vulnerable. They must let go of their ego, try new things, and experiment. This requires them to *rethink deeply held beliefs that drive the way they behave. And ultimately do what it takes to change.*

After 'I go' is 'we go'. The change the leader is making is really for the people they're leading, therefore it's natural to involve them in the process. The leader should ask them for suggestions and then genuinely consider these suggestions. Being important to the coworkers, they should be important to the leader as well. Leaders should admit that they are not perfect and work to demonstrate growth in their leadership.

*After 'I go' and 'we go', there is 'let's go'.*

'Let's go' means that leaders need to collate their own ideas with the suggestions from their coworkers and then determine what goes into their action plan. Once the action plan is set, they should implement it together with their coworkers. This makes it all the more obvious that leadership is really about cocreating change with coworkers.

Clearly, it's about we-centered leadership creating behaviors that are more effective; over time, they become new habits that the leader uses and coworkers adopt—a new way of working within the organization. Sometimes that mini-process, called SOP (Standard Operating Procedure), is very explicit. Sometimes it's much more implicit and embedded in the organizational or team culture.

So conceptually, this should all be very clear and simple. We know that leaders who are we-centered focus on 'I go, we go, and let's go', and more than 95% become more effective in the eyes of their coworkers. So that basically means guaranteed success.

Reflecting on what I just shared, let's discuss what you see as me- and we-centered leadership in your environment.

Here is a question to get us started: When a leader is very me-centered, what does their behavior look like?

**Sanjiv:** Well, these leaders are not very good at listening to others. They might be autocratic in their decisions or even indecisive. They could be focused on power and control and possibly be micromanagers. I've seen how they quickly blame others or make excuses when things aren't going as planned. They might be very political or self-serving in the way they act in the organization.

**Will:** Yes, it doesn't require a lot of imagination, does it? It just requires jogging your memory of what you have seen other people doing. Then let's look at the other side of that. When leaders are very we-centered, what are the behaviors that those leaders display?

**Sanjiv:** They're really good at goal-setting and doing that together with their team. They're very clear on the direction the team needs to go. They basically include others in the goal-setting connected to the strategy to provide a solid direction for all individually and collectively.

Then they work together with the team towards those goals. They involve people in the discussions. They involve people in decision-making. They work to make these decisions together. They think and plan ahead. And also, they walk their talk. They're good at bringing people along, and at the same time, they are decisive.

They're eager to share their feelings and how they think about things. They ask people how they think about things, and they ask others to speak up. They're good at rewarding and recognizing others for their achievements. They're good at collaboration. Should I go on? I can talk about this for much longer.

**Will:** Yeah, I think we have a good picture now of what me- and we-centered behavior looks like. So, knowing that 95% of we-centered leaders will change from the perspective of their coworkers, on a scale of one to 10 (one being very me-centered and 10 being very we-centered), where do you want to commit to as a leader throughout this leadership coaching engagement?

**Sanjiv:** Yes, it is clear I want to commit to being a 9.5 out of 10.

**Will:** Thanks Sanjiv, that is fantastic. Then, since you want me to be your coach and keep you on track, would you allow me to point out to you when you're not the 9.5 that you'd like to be?

**Sanjiv:** Yes, of course. That is what I need from you; that is why I am working with you.

Typically, most leaders come with numbers like 8, 9, and 10, and some overachieving type-A personalities want to be at 12. We have a good chuckle at that. But it sets a clear tone in the engagement, and it locks in their commitment. That is what you want and what they need.

In this short conversation, Sanjiv and I created the far view, the destination of the coaching engagement. We created the value that the leader gets throughout the journey. And we established the mindset and behaviors that create a safe and easy path to making that value a reality.

And throughout this conversation, you might have noted that I didn't really push the leader in any way. I just guided the conversation. Let them talk; let them find the right answers themselves.

# HOW 2 – AGILE MAKES IT EASY

Here, we actually lean into some of the agile principles that most clients apply in their own organization when they manage improvements in service quality, supply chain, production, safety, IT, and various other parts of the organization. An agile work approach, typically used in project management, emphasizes focus, collaboration, adaptability, and iterative improvement involving stakeholders through asking for feedback and suggestions. We integrate the agile principles of focus, incremental change, and help from coworkers into the leadership space. Because they also use them in other parts of the organization, it is easy for the leader to accept the usefulness and truthfulness of these principles. That creates automatic acceptance of an easy and safe way to manage their leadership journey.

Let's go back to the conversation with Sanjiv.

**Will:** So, Sanjiv. In your organization, you're responsible for financial services and the improvement of the quality of those services. I'm sure you're familiar with agile principles of incremental change. They're all about focusing on what you want to change and making the change process incremental, step-by-step, to deliver value quickly and solicit help from the stakeholders around you, like coworkers, customers, and other parties. You're familiar with such agile approaches, right?

**Sanjiv:** Of course I'm familiar with that. I love agile.

**Will:** Fabulous. We apply the same agile principles in leadership change. As we proceed in the coaching journey, would you be okay to focus on two areas of change that are important to you and the coworkers you work with? Ask these coworkers for some suggestions on what they think would be helpful for that change from their perspective. Then make an action plan to create an incremental implementation of that change over time, so that on a month-by-month basis, you see how this whole change comes into reality step by step. This would take less than five minutes per day. It happens in the flow of work, with no extra time required. Would you be okay to use that same agile approach in your leadership change?

**Sanjiv:** Well, that makes all logical sense and I am keen to see how to apply these principles in leadership change. It looks like the coaching has become 'Project Me'.

**Will:** Wonderful. Actually, you will see that it will be 'Project We'. Because the more you focus on what is important to you *and* your coworkers, the more they will be involved in making the required change with you. Very agile, as you will notice.

Taking this approach in the conversation with leaders makes it easy for them to embrace the coaching approach, as it feels logical, familiar, and acceptable to them. A picture is worth a thousand words: You can see some live demonstrations in the eLearning resources at the end of this chapter.

At this point, with all the decision-makers committed to helping the leader get better (start smart), and with the leader committed (WHY) to the journey and their destination, the journey can start. Its success hinges on three factors: focus, structure, and help. We will look at these factors one by one in the next chapters. The first step is to articulate the main theme of the coaching journey for the leader to improve.

# ELEARNING RESOURCES

Chapter resources and demos are available in your eLearning account. Sign up and access it here: www.globalcoachgroup.com/triplewinbook or email coach@globalcoachgroup.com

CHAPTER 6

# FOCUS CHANGES EVERYTHING

Focus makes change simple – WHAT

# THE UNSTOPPABLE POWER OF FOCUSED CHANGE

Picture a magnifying glass concentrating the sun's rays on a single point, igniting a fire. Most successful behavioral change programs aimed at disorders around gambling, shopping, eating, internet, smoking, alcohol, etc., have a single focus for success. That's the power of focus we're aiming to achieve in our coaching approach: All efforts and actions converge on two goals, resulting in meaningful improvements for leaders and their teams.

By the end of this chapter, you'll know exactly how to find and articulate the right leadership behaviors for the leader to work on. In our approach, we help leaders select two areas of focus, which become the hinges of change for everything else as well. Focus ensures that the leaders keep their eyes on the prize.

When you map out a larger leadership business case for the leader, they will see not just two things changing; they'll see that their whole life as a leader is changing as a result of their focus. And when they work on what matters to coworkers, then the map of change just widens further.

Let me tell you why this type of focus is so important:

• Leaders are busy, and they don't have time to focus on many things to change. Believe me, I've seen it happen all over the world. When people focus on too many things to change, they succeed at some, fail at others, and consequently feel discouraged. In their performance appraisals, their managers talk about the latter, instead of celebrating the successes they've had.

- If the leader realizes that changing two things changes everything, *they don't need to try to change everything*. That is a very powerful understanding to have. Leaders get this quickly because in many other parts of the organization where improvements are required—for example, in IT, research, supply chain, manufacturing, marketing, and safety management—a similar logic of focusing on a bottleneck is used.

- If the leader can rally themselves and their coworkers around their focus of change, it becomes impossible not to make measurable and meaningful improvements in those areas. When everyone pushes in the same direction, they make an impact.

When it comes to setting goals and priorities, leaders in organizations often face the challenge of making decisions based on their own insights as well as those of other stakeholders. To navigate this, it's common for teams to divide their efforts, spreading focus across multiple goals and priorities to achieve their objectives. However, it's well understood that many successful change systems emphasize the power of concentrating on just one or two key objectives. This focus fosters commitment and drives meaningful change within the organization. We embrace this philosophy in our coaching methodology, applying it through the following three steps.

# DEFINE THE RIGHT FOCUS IN THREE STEPS

Most leaders have plenty of improvement areas to choose from, but selecting those that are important to all parties—to the leader, their coworkers, and their manager—is essential to ensuring collaboration and mutual support throughout the change process. Here's how to establish the right focus in a structured and effective manner.

## 1. Feedback

Select 5 to 15 coworkers and interview them individually for 15 to 30 minutes using the following questions:

- What are the leader's strengths?

- What are the leader's areas to develop?

- What environments bring out the best in the leader?

- What environments bring out the worst in the leader?

I've done this many times. After the first few interviews, you're thinking, 'I have no idea where this is going and what the real issues are.' But after you've talked to eight or so people, you're thinking, 'It is so obvious what this person's challenges really are.' Then, in the subsequent interviews, you find consistent confirmation of these themes.

What you need to do next is to basically compile the interview content into a report by grouping the answers to all four questions into two sections: *strengths* and *areas to develop*. There are plenty of ways to do this, but I'm going to share with you my favorite way to compile a report:

- Keep it as verbatim as possible, as your editing might distort the meaning of the answers that coworkers gave, leading to confusing discussions with the leader later on.

- Limit the report to two pages of strengths and two pages of areas to develop. The logic here is very simple: The objective of your behavioral interview report is for the leader to pick two areas for leadership growth moving forward—it is not to provide a comprehensive leadership effectiveness analysis. Furthermore, it is much easier to pick two things from a shorter list than from a longer list. I recommend compiling a short list of maybe the 5 to 10 most important areas to develop instead of a long laundry list over many pages.

You can make this process more sophisticated and elaborate, if you like, by asking for examples to illustrate the answers coworkers are providing. This would likely require you to extend interview times to up to one hour. You can also amplify this approach by using an online 360 assessment. (We most often use our Global Leadership Assessment GLA360.) A 360 assessment provides a high level of rigor and more objectivity in the collected feedback.

Whichever approach you are excited about is likely a good approach at this point. This reminds me of the quote from Deng Xiaoping: 'It's not about black cats or white cats; it's about cats that catch mice.'

# 2. Funnel

I find it helpful to be very clear about the objectives in every part of the coaching journey. The debrief meeting with the leader has the single objective of helping the leader select two areas of leadership growth based on the feedback provided in the report. Although many coaching engagements are initiated to help leaders in areas they want to improve, a good leadership development effort must aim at improvement in areas that impact others. This is why leadership growth should focus on what others have said are the top strengths and areas to develop.

### *Introducing the feedback report: Setting the right tone for openness*

Typically, receiving feedback brings a little anxiety. Putting the leader at ease and helping them to open their mind is super-helpful at this stage. You can explain to them how you went about doing the interviews; who was involved; and how collaborative, open, and forthcoming people have been in providing the information in the report. Here you can emphasize that anonymity was guaranteed to the people who participated and that you will continue to respect that as you talk them through the report.

Furthermore, you can emphasize to the leader that the report's objective is not to offer a comprehensive, in-depth analysis of their leadership competencies and abilities—it is to select two areas for leadership change that are important to them and their coworkers. This sets the right tone for the leader to engage constructively with the report's content, fostering a genuine commitment to personal improvement.

*Then hand the report to the leader, saying: 'Read the next two pages of strengths and then tell me what you think.'*

You can get a sense of how the leader is processing the information by watching how they interact with the report. Are they studying it intently? Taking notes? Skimming and brushing it aside? Their behavior will tell you a great deal about how to conduct the debrief.

Once they finish, say again: 'Tell me what you think.'

The phrasing of this is important. At this stage, you are simply giving the leader space to respond. Because feedback reports can be emotionally charged for some, you can help yourself by appealing to their thinking rather than inquiring about their emotions. This phrasing prompts the leader to respond with their thoughts about the feedback, which gives you valuable insight into their thought process and how well they understood the main themes.

*After debriefing the strengths, use the same approach to review areas to develop on the next two pages.*

The leader will likely exhibit a range of behaviors and emotions, from discomfort, disbelief, or outright upset on the one hand, to empathy for their coworkers on the other. This is to be expected. Because your aim right now is simply to give the leader space to respond, any response that connects the main themes is acceptable. Let the leader talk for a few minutes about their thoughts on the areas to develop. Once you feel they have exhausted what they want to say and understood the main themes, it is time to briefly summarize the report.

Ask, 'What insights did you gain from the behavioral interviews report?'

Now that the leader has read through the report and expressed their response to the feedback, it is time to distill the main strengths and areas to develop from the behavioral interviews report. This summary discussion should be brief and concise. Questions to ask would be:

- What did others say are your strengths?

- What specific behaviors are a part of that?

- What did others say are your areas to develop?

- What specific behaviors are a part of that?

# 3. Focus

If time and the emotions of the leader allow, it is good to let the leader select the two leadership growth areas they want to focus on moving forward. I personally make it a point to let the leader choose these leadership growth areas in the same session. After all the feedback and the emotional turmoil they have been going through, picking these leadership growth areas gives them both a sense of relief and a sense of moving forward. Typically, this gives a huge boost to their emotional setting, and they will leave the meeting on an energetic high.

More often than not, they talk to a coworker or their manager about their feedback session immediately after the coaching session; I want their reaction to be: 'Wow, the time today with my coach was a great and tough session, because I went through a lot of feedback and my head was kind of spinning. However, I selected two things that I think are really important to my team and me, and I think I have the key in my hand to unlock further success and leadership potential. This was a great meeting, and my coach guided me so well through this feedback process.'

Just as important, by taking this approach, you have created that triple buy-in—from the leader, the manager, and the coworkers—in whatever leadership growth areas that the leader will select. Leaders tend to feel that they are alone in this situation, which is why we share with them our list of frequently selected leadership growth areas. By doing this, two things happen:

- They realize that the challenge they face is common to many other successful leaders.

- It helps them to articulate their leadership growth areas well and embrace these moving forward.

You can download a complete list of the leadership growth areas most frequently selected by leaders based on feedback from the eLearning at the end of this chapter.

# BUILD THE BROADER BUSINESS CASE AROUND THE FOCUS (THE RIPPLE EFFECT OF LEADERSHIP CHANGE FOR ALL COWORKERS)

## Focus on a burning platform

A burning platform is a critical situation that unites everyone around a clear need for change, offering an overwhelming array of benefits as a result. Examples would be green energy projects or the use of recycled materials in products. In leadership change, the burning platform is the two areas of development with a triple buy-in (leader, coworker, and manager) for which you can make a convincing business case. The truth is that most people change if two conditions are present.

The first condition is that the aforementioned burning platform truly exists. People need to be adequately convinced of the need for change. You create conviction through your feedback debrief. The second condition is that significant benefits can be enjoyed after the change occurs. These benefits must be important to the leader and important to the coworkers who are important to the leader, and they must be numerous enough to keep focus and motivation high.

Before you dive into the business case for leadership change, work with the leader on a personal example. Ask them to think about a time when they set a goal and achieved it. They most likely had a specific benefit or outcome in mind when they started that journey. Did they get that benefit? More importantly, did they get just one benefit, or did they find many other benefits that improved other aspects of their life at the same time?

## Personal example: Illustrating benefits of change

I often use this personal example with my clients to illustrate the application of the benefits of change. Many years ago, I had my annual feedback from my doctor on my medical health assessment. From the long list of data in this report, there were two dozen areas that I could have chosen to improve (e.g. lose weight, build muscle, drink less coffee). My cholesterol had been creeping up consistently in the years before that and was now at levels that required serious consideration for change. The trendline was in the wrong direction, and based on historical data, there were no downward inflection points in sight.

I chose cholesterol as my area for change. Together with my doctor, I made a long list of benefits that I would gain from lowering my cholesterol: better blood pressure, living longer, better eating habits, more exercise, sleeping better, more energy, higher endurance, more activity time with my children and future grandchildren, quicker recovery from minor illnesses, higher resistance to infections, better skin quality, better food choices for me and my family, lower medical bills, etc.

In your coaching, feel free to use this example. Or you can share a story of your own. The key is to focus on someone facing a big life change with enthusiasm and positivity once they realize just how much they stand to gain by confidently proceeding. The leader should see themselves in the story and you will respond by helping them see the benefits for themselves and others when positive change happens. Take leadership over the areas the leader has selected and work with them to compile a list of the benefits of improving in these areas. The benefits then collectively become an extensive business case for the leader, their coworkers, and the organization.

## Triple Win Business Case for Change

Change doesn't happen in isolation. When a positive change occurs in one area, other areas are positively affected in tandem. These 'splash benefits' can make achievement even more satisfying when looking in the rear-view mirror. But what happens when benefits are contemplated before taking the first step? The answer is simple: Each additional benefit makes change easier.

Do not forget that leaders are accustomed to justifying new ideas by defining their business benefits. This is called creating a business case, and it includes a high-level view of the benefits, costs, and investments required. In the context of executive coaching, a business case lists the benefits that the leader and coworkers get as a result of improving in their leadership growth areas—and how it impacts organizational performance. We call this the Triple Win Business Case for Better Teams, Better Leaders, and Better Results. The Triple Win Business Case exercise encourages the leader to momentarily think selfishly while also thinking altruistically, considering their own gain as well as the gain others get through their efforts to change.

# THE LEADER'S PATH FORWARD

At this stage, the leader has identified two critical leadership growth areas that are important both to themselves and their coworkers, for example, disciplined execution and empowerment. They have created a clear business case, outlining the benefits of their growth for themselves and their team. The leader now sees the light at the end of the tunnel, and they know it is not an approaching train: It is the light into their new season of leadership, their solution to their likely long-standing leadership challenges.

Leaders understand the WHAT, that cocreating change with coworkers makes sense, as the latter will provide further suggestions. They know that it also makes sense to their manager and their coworkers. They have a goal, plan, path, and guide assisting them on their journey. This makes them excited to move forward. However, to successfully navigate this path, the HOW, they need structure.

In the next chapter, that's what we will explore: how structure helps leaders navigate their change as they progress on this transformative journey.

# ELEARNING RESOURCES

Chapter resources and demos are available in your eLearning account. Sign up and access it here: www.globalcoachgroup.com/triplewinbook or email coach@globalcoachgroup.com

# CHAPTER 7

# STRUCTURE IS FREEDOM

Structure makes change easy – HOW

# EMBRACING THE COMFORT OF STRUCTURE

With the leadership focus defining the WHAT, the challenge for the leader has become really simple. They know they don't have to change everything, just two things. These could be very straightforward things, such as *more disciplined implementation* and *involving others in decision-making*. The next key to success now is making simple *easy*.

Whereas focus makes change simple, embracing the comfort of structure makes simplicity 'easy', as it consistently yields results. Structure is the road to success, as defined in the business case. In daily life, people depend on structures to accomplish tasks (e.g. using one's daily commute routine for work). Routines and habits are familiar to the brain and encourage low-effort execution and efficiency.

During times of change, however, a leader's usual routine becomes disrupted. Offering a tried-and-true structure as a coach provides comfort for the leader in the change process, much as a car's navigation system guides you to your destination. Reliable structure assures the client that the change will lead to the success outlined in their business case.

## The power of structure with your personal fitness trainer

I will never forget the year I worked with my friend Philip as my personal trainer. A powerlifting champion in the UK, Philip had transitioned into training high-net-worth individuals. His success lay in using a structured approach, one applying proven fitness principles as building blocks for programs he could tailor to his clients' unique needs.

Philip and I began with a thorough health assessment, and he helped me define my personalized goals. Based on that, he crafted a training and nutrition plan tailored specifically for me. I also got a serious workout in my very first session, which made me feel that momentum was building that same day. The great thing was that his structured approach led to early results, which fostered new habits and behaviors that accelerated my progress.

As I progressed through the regimen, I witnessed steady improvement each week. This consistent success reinforced my motivation and commitment to the process. Philip's ability to combine customization with foundational principles allowed him to expedite change in each client based on their individual needs and starting point. He also minimized distractions that could derail progress.

Philip was a very hands-on trainer. His strategic approach ensured I clearly recognized the impact of my daily choices on my long-term fitness goals. This further reinforced the effectiveness of the underlying structure upon which he had built my plan.

For instance, one day I was going to treat myself to a candy bar after a great workout. Philip noticed this and asked me to read the nutritional facts on the wrapper and tell him the number of calories in my self-awarded prize. I was amazed to read 185 calories and hesitantly shared this with Philip, fearing what his response would be. With his big persona and his soft yet determined voice, he explained how eating the candy bar would add 185 calories to my count, which would negatively impact my current achievement in the session I had just finished. He said, 'This is a great moment of choice. Eat the candy bar and get back on your machine of choice and burn off the extra 185 calories, or enjoy your achievement as you go and shower.' I quickly calculated that this would add another 20 minutes to my workout, and I already felt tired. I ditched the candy bar and felt good about it.

On another occasion, I had a problem with pain in one of my knees, which impacted my running pace that day. Philip noticed that I was not exercising at my usual intensity level. After asking a few questions, he suggested I try the rowing machine, which would relieve the pressure on my knee while providing the same cardiac workout and calorie burn.

These coaching moments and micro-adjustments made a big difference. Working with Philip was a powerful reminder that relying on a proven, adaptable structure applies far beyond fitness. It is a model that can enable coaches to ensure success for their clients. Just as Philip leverages foundational fitness principles into customized plans that deliver results, coaches can rely on a structured methodology tailored to each leader. When clients experience steady improvement, it reinforces their commitment and motivation to reach their goals and create their 'new me'.

## The benefits of structure in coaching service delivery

Structured coaching service delivery offers reliability, time efficiency, predictability, and high-quality results. The structured approach doesn't negate customization; rather, it provides room for refinement and adaptation to individual clients' needs or specific goals. It also allows for freedom and experimentation during the coaching service. Flexibility empowers coaches to enhance the coaching journey with additional tools and elements, much like decorating a Christmas tree.

Some leaders and clients may resist a structured approach, associating it with a lack of bespoke solutions; in fact, it reduces doubt and anxiety and boosts confidence for both the coach and the leader. Structure and customization can definitely coexist.

## Navigating change with structure

In change management, relying on structure is crucial for success. The eight-step organizational change model of Harvard professor John Kotter has been used by many organizations since it was first published in 1996. That structure creates alignment and momentum and allows the tracking of change results. I tried it myself as company CEO earlier in my career, with amazing results. One of my main conclusions was that structure takes the guesswork out of change and aligns people to work together toward success. Change always introduces unfamiliar environments, and having a reliable structure acts as the much-needed guide, easing discomfort and providing support. A structured approach also enables experimentation within a secure framework, allowing change to happen gradually.

And with the steady hand of an expert coach guiding leaders through a proven approach, it all goes much easier and allows people to enjoy their change journey.

Consider the analogy of using navigation apps while driving in unfamiliar territory. Good directions are a kind of structure that ensures a safe and efficient journey. When traveling, I often rent cars to visit customers or explore the country. Driving in unfamiliar traffic environments in the Middle East, the USA, Europe, Australia, and Africa has challenged me to adapt my driving style according to local rules. Do in Rome as the Romans do. During these experiences, navigational tools like Google Maps or Waze have provided structure and guidance, alleviating the discomfort that comes with the unknown.

With them, I can focus on being present, enjoying the moment, and experiencing the journey without concern. I don't need to stress about the next turn or whether I'll arrive on time. Even if I make a wrong turn or decide to explore something in a different direction, I can trust navigation systems to bring me back on track and adapt my journey, while informing me about the impact on arrival time. Such support is invaluable, allowing me to prioritize what's most important and valuable at any given time. It's a case of structure creating immense, worry-free freedom.

## Magic, cooking, and coaching:
## A structured comparison

Examining the structured approach in magic or cooking, exemplified by following the instructions of a great magician or the recipe of a renowned chef, reveals that structure brings comfort to unfamiliar situations. These experienced professionals may appear to improvise, but their success is rooted in their meticulously thought-out structures. This structured process, while not always apparent, ensures consistent success.

And structure doesn't have to feel rigid; it can feel like magic. I literally mean magic. When my kids were younger, I did card tricks for younger audiences in community programs. Everyone loves magic, especially children, and it is a great way to tell a story and engage the audience. But we all know that magic is not really *magic*. It is the meticulous execution of a series of actions that must be carefully choreographed and implemented—which then *looks* like magic.

I was working in London a few years ago with a group of coaches in our certification program. During a break, I was walking in the hotel lobby, where I saw two magicians sitting at a table. One of them was teaching the other how to perfect a card trick. He specifically pointed out to the novice magician how to position his index finger on the deck of cards. The success or failure of the trick depended on a few millimeters of movement by that finger.

It brought me back to my magic days, reminding me that micro-changes can make a big difference—and that relying on structure and execution makes it all look like magic.

With coaching, it's no different. If you implement your coaching service using a structured approach based on the client's needs, then you know what you need to do *now*—and what you need to do *next*—to produce the intended results. But just as with magic, the client doesn't know the structure; they are journeying with you to experience the change and achieve their results. What looks like magic to them feels like structure for you. It is a customized service specifically tailored to their needs. And that's what really matters.

We all love a good meal and enjoy eating delicious food. One of the most famous chefs in the world is the Englishman Jamie Oliver. Jamie comes across as very informal and friendly in his cooking style, giving the impression that he invents ideas on the spot and throws everything together effortlessly to create an amazing dish. However, when you study Jamie's recipes, published for anyone to use, you'll see that they are meticulously structured, with detailed preparations of all ingredients, lists of the equipment needed, and step-by-step instructions. Even if you're not a great cook, you can create fantastic meals that look and taste as if they were created by a master chef. I am not a great cook, but all the meals I've made using Jamie's recipes turn out to be delicious and make my guests applaud my cooking skills.

This might seem contradictory to Jamie's casual cooking style, but the reality is that Jamie's cooking is backed by a structured and well-thought-out process. Just like a magician, he knows exactly what he's doing, why he's doing it, and how he's doing it. Despite his seemingly jovial approach, he caters to the specific requirements to create a great dish.

In our coaching approach, we have been doing exactly that. Let's look at the structure first, and then we'll do the magic later.

## Key ingredients of a successful coaching structure

Similar to a delicious meal or magical performance, the key ingredients for a coaching service structured for success are:

1. Use agile principles to implement incremental change.

2. Involve coworkers to cocreate change and make change visible.

3. Create solutions proactively: Work with leaders to devise solutions for potential challenges.

These ingredients work harmoniously and are woven into the structured framework for change. The leader's action plan, focusing on daily behaviors, serves as a customized checklist, enhancing the flow toward results. This structured approach accelerates the achievement of goals, making the coaching service more effective.

You will see that structure is not the enemy of creativity or customization; instead, structure fosters a fertile environment where creativity and customization can thrive. By embracing structure, coaches empower their clients to navigate change successfully and achieve their desired outcomes. Let me show you how this works and how it makes coaching easy. And remember, as with magic tricks and great meals, you will not necessarily recognize the individual ingredients as they seamlessly integrate into the coaching service.

## Agile change makes momentum easy

In its simplest form, agile change focuses on creating an action plan for change and assessing its impact. This involves considering what works well, what creates results, what feels comfortable, and what has the right impact. The process also considers difficulties in implementing the action plan, areas not working well, and elements causing confusion or friction. After this reflection, the focus shifts to doing things differently in creating an improved action plan, with reduced friction to address obstacles and increased traction that further builds momentum—all contributing to a continuous, step-by-step change process leading to tangible results.

As leaders embark on the journey of change, they often encounter what we refer to as the 'challenge of change'. Despite possessing numerous strengths that have contributed to their success, leaders may find that overusing these strengths becomes an obstacle to becoming a truly great and inspirational leader for whom people want to work. As part of our approach, we use a framework called Good, Difficult, Different (GDD), which serves as a method for reflecting on and improving the action plan within an agile framework. You can access that resource via the resources section at the end of this chapter.

## Involving coworkers makes perception change easy

The challenge for leaders lies not only in making a change. It is also about maintaining momentum, creating new habits, and embodying that change to become the 'new me' they want to be; additionally, they need to ensure that their coworkers notice that 'new me'. If the leader has changed and improved, but the coworkers don't notice, then that improvement doesn't really exist.

Perceptions are resilient. Consumer goods companies know this all too well: They undertake extensive efforts, using advertising and promotions in all their forms, to show the value of improved products. They know that if consumers fail to notice that improvement, then there is no value in it. We have learned how to apply this truth about perceptions in leadership, making change visible in ways easy for coworkers to recognize and value.

First, it's important to recognize that people's perceptions are indeed resilient, making it essential for leaders to persist in demonstrating change and showing their new ways of being. That takes effort and time. Other people's perceptions can be tough to change; it's easier for individuals to remain steadfast in their existing beliefs based on past experiences. People resist changing their opinions/perceptions unless there is overwhelming new evidence over a significant period of time.

Don't forget that individuals in the workplace are not actively observing the leader's change efforts. People are focused on their own agendas and problem-solving during meetings and working through their daily to-do lists. Their attention is not devoted to evaluating the leader's evolving behaviors. More important things capture their attention than whether the leader has been more decisive than a month ago.

Imagine we're in the realm of consumer goods, specifically carbonated drinks. Think of the variety—colas, flavored drinks, and more. Now, consider the critical question: Who determines whether such carefully branded drinks are perceived as delicious? It's the consumers who are the ultimate decision-makers. If they find a particular product satisfying, they return to buy more. Conversely, if the experience falls short, they abandon that brand and shift their allegiance to another product, likely from a competitor company. Consumers vote with their feet, and that's a powerful indicator of a brand's success or failure.

Now, let's transpose this consumer-driven decision-making into the organizational landscape, specifically in the context of leaders and their coworkers. Just as consumers determine the success of a brand, coworkers play a pivotal role in determining the effectiveness of a leader within the organization. They decide whether the leader is effective, just as consumers decide on the success of a product. If coworkers appreciate and resonate with a leader, they remain committed and engaged, just like consumers continuing to purchase their favorite drink. However, if dissatisfaction sets in, coworkers, like consumers, explore other opportunities. The shrewdest among them (like the smartest consumers) are often the first to make a move. And where do these coworkers go? They go to the competition.

This story highlights a fundamental truth: To manage change effectively, it is essential to recognize that, like consumers, coworkers play a vital role in determining the effectiveness of a leader. They, too, vote with their feet, either by staying committed to their current workplace or seeking opportunities elsewhere. The best and smartest people leave first.

Perceptions can be challenging to manage; they necessitate active involvement from coworkers to cocreate the change and make it visible and impactful. This is a powerful strategy to gain momentum and reduce friction. Involving coworkers ensures that their opinions and suggestions are considered in the action plan, making the change more relevant to them and thus more effective.

This collaborative approach not only accelerates the change process but also fosters commitment from coworkers, as they become integral participants in the decision-making and execution of the change. By incorporating this into the structure, integrating coworkers into the change process aligns with the key success factors of creating traction, reducing friction, and ensuring visibility in the coaching process.

In summary, the consistent step-by-step change process, combined with involving coworkers in cocreating change, forms dynamic and adaptable ingredients in the coaching service. They become a set of modules and tools that can be rearranged like Lego blocks to suit the needs of both the coach and the client.

## Create solutions proactively, which encourages leaders to devise solutions for potential challenges

Without exception, as leaders travel on their coaching journey to success, they face various challenges. Sometimes, challenges are of a business nature and have nothing to do with their leadership or coaching; for example, they may get involved in projects that absorb a lot of their attention. These challenges throw up roadblocks, creating friction that can slow down the coaching journey. The coach needs to address that friction to maintain pace and progress.

My coaching with Diane illustrates this point too well. Diane had been an accomplished senior executive in a global IT firm. Some six months into the coaching journey, Diane faced significant obstacles with a major global account project. This issue had eroded the trust between her, her manager, and some of the team members, posing a substantial challenge to her leadership role.

As part of the coaching journey, Diane focused on more disciplined project management with her team, and an important question arose: How could she continue her coaching and leadership journey while facing the current trust challenge? Feeling deflated and overwhelmed, Diane was considering giving coaching up altogether or pausing it for a few months.

These scenarios are far from unique in coaching engagements. As coaches, our role is to help leaders navigate these challenges and consider solutions. The challenge is that these problems can seem so overwhelming that it is difficult for leaders to envision a way out. In our coaching service, we include a solution that has always worked in such cases. Let me describe it.

During the coaching session, we revisited Diane's Triple Win Business Case, articulated earlier in her coaching journey. As she read through the business case, she highlighted the value her leadership change would bring to herself, her team, and the business. These were all things that were dear to her—personal benefits she had committed to her coworkers and value she knew the business needed. Reflecting on these still-valid truths reignited her motivation and aspiration, resulting in renewed focus. It also helped her see the connection between the erosion of trust that had occurred, her leadership focus on disciplined execution, and the overall business case. It all came back together for her; it all made sense.

Through this vital discussion, Diane realized that the trust issues she was facing and the problems she needed to resolve required disciplined implementation and the power of cocreation with her coworkers. Rather than giving up on her coaching journey, Diane chose to double down on her efforts, embracing disciplined execution and involving her coworkers in the process. Ultimately, this approach helped her foster trust, improve her leadership effectiveness, and achieve the vision she had set for herself and her team.

It's essential for coaches to create solutions proactively for problems that are bound to arise. Encourage your clients to stay focused, involve their team members, and work together towards success. Fostering a structured and disciplined approach can pave the way for a transformative coaching journey that inspires leaders to overcome challenges and reach their full potential.

Using the Triple Win Business Case is just one example of many guiding tools in coaching. Most problems that leaders face during their coaching journey can be anticipated, and proactive strategies can be created to solve them. We reverse-engineered this into the coaching structure, with the clients generating solutions to potential problems before they occur. This helps leaders identify the problems in the first place and apply solutions they have created themselves, leading to a higher level of commitment.

Creating solutions proactively doesn't necessarily reduce the size or importance of a problem. However, it helps the leader realize that they possess the tools and capabilities to overcome these challenges. They have already committed to their own solutions, which increases the likelihood of successful problem resolution. In essence, creating solutions proactively helps leaders confidently tackle challenges on their coaching journey. Proactively and collaboratively creating solutions strengthens the coaching partnership, ensures a smoother journey, and fosters a strong sense of ownership in overcoming obstacles.

## To sum up: Structure makes success easy

Navigating a coaching engagement can be challenging. There can be confusion and uncertainty about the direction of the leader's journey. The key to overcoming this is something we've talked about before: relying on a structured approach and modular elements that can be adapted to fit the leader's needs. By strategically mixing and matching these modules, a coach can create a tailored framework that ensures success both for the leader and the coach. This approach provides the essential stepping stones for larger success in your coaching practice, offering a scalable process that can be replicated across different clients and organizations. Such efficiency not only simplifies the proposition for clients but facilitates quick and effective communication, allowing coaches to present proposals in just 15 to 20 minutes.

Presenting the coaching service as a comprehensive approach that consistently delivers results should be part of your sales conversations with clients. Some may raise objections, fearing that structure hampers customization and creativity. However, the truth is quite the opposite. A proven structure serves as a fireproof pathway to success, allowing room for creativity and customization. The more effectively one operates using this structure and creates progress with the leader, the greater the opportunity to explore creative solutions along the way. Instead of undermining results, this approach adds more value.

Having employed this approach for over 25 years, I've found that structure enhances effectiveness. Effectiveness creates additional time for more coaching tailored to the leader's needs, for example, problem-solving specific challenges they have with their team or manager, defining their personal leadership model, and doing personality or career assessments to gain more awareness and insight for themselves. These are the kind of activities leaders deeply appreciate and recognize as extra value from you as their coach.

At times, people push back on the concept of incremental change. It is essential to remind them that this step-by-step approach mirrors successful practices in various business domains, whether they are managing supply chains, software development, safety, product development, or scientific research studies.

The structured approach not only allows for experimentation and iteration but also provides a rinse-and-repeat capability, which is crucial for scalability. Unlike a fully customized environment, a structured approach permits the creation of a repeatable process, facilitating collaboration with other coaches and serving a broader client base. This methodology aligns with how professionals in other fields, such as doctors and lawyers, handle highly customized yet structured environments to consistently achieve high-quality outcomes.

## Structure fosters freedom

Consider some of the analogies we've looked at, such as driving in new cities, cooking meals, and performing magic. In a similar vein, coaching can be likened to having a personal navigator guiding you through your leadership journey. A structured coaching approach guided by an experienced coach creates a sense of comfort throughout the process. Just as a GPS system relieves stress during unfamiliar travels, a structured coaching program enables you to be present in each moment, confident that your leader will arrive at their desired destination, becoming a more effective leader, growing their team, and achieving better performance results.

In conclusion, the key takeaway is understanding that structure fosters freedom. This freedom enables coaches to be creative, experiment, and iterate the coaching journey for the leader. It's through this structured experimentation that sustainable success is achieved.

Now, as we delve into mobilizing help around the leader, we'll uncover how this structured approach not only benefits the leader but also enhances the entire team and, consequently, their performance results.

# ELEARNING RESOURCES

Chapter resources and demos are available in your eLearning account. Sign up and access it here: www.globalcoachgroup.com/triplewinbook or email coach@globalcoachgroup.com

CHAPTER 8

# HELP IS ALL AROUND

Help makes change speedy – HOW

# ASKING FOR HELP IS A SIGN OF STRENGTH

The best leaders are not those who have all the right answers but the ones who draw on the help and expertise of others. In this age of knowledge workers, business leaders involve their teams and coworkers in problem-solving all the time, whether the issue relates to product improvement, marketing, or hiring new employees.

Help is readily available in our organizations. When we seek help from managers, team members, and other types of coworkers, we are leveraging their expertise and experience. Leaders tend to focus their leadership development on areas that are important to them; as they do so, their team members are generally willing to help, support, and invest in the leader. This often includes peers who are internal customers—they also stand ready to help and support leaders to be more successful. So help is all around.

We talked about focus and structure earlier. These factors help make leadership change simple and easy. Asking for help speeds up change for the simple reason that now we're rallying the troops, and everybody is on board to cocreate change together.

The data supporting the involvement of coworkers in the coaching process is indeed compelling. When coworkers are not part of the coaching journey, only 18% acknowledge the leader's improvement. However, this acknowledgment escalates dramatically to an impressive 95% when coworkers are actively involved in the coaching journey. This shift represents more than a fivefold enhancement in results. Indeed, what leader wouldn't be thrilled to achieve over five times the impact in any aspect of their leadership? This return on investment ultimately benefits not only the leader but also their team and the performance results. When you consider that involving coworkers in the coaching journey doesn't require much time or effort from the leader being coached, it really is a no-brainer. (The truth is that involving coworkers does not require *any* extra time from the leader; I will show you why later in this chapter.)

Other independent research supports these findings. Stanford Business School lecturer and *New York Times* bestselling author Shirzad Chamine has trained more than 45,000 coaches on Positive Intelligence. His research findings indicate that positive new habits supported by accountability partners have a 500% increased likelihood of success compared to working without a support system.

It's clear that coworkers play a valuable role in helping leaders improve more quickly, positively impacting their own improvement, team effectiveness, and performance results. By involving coworkers in the coaching, leaders can expect to achieve more significant and lasting improvement in their leadership abilities, benefiting the entire organization. This always reminds me of the African proverb: 'If you want to go fast, go alone. If you want to go far, go together.' And going together is exactly what we're now doing in our leadership coaching process.

With the knowledge that coworkers add significant value to the leader in their leadership and coaching journey, we can move from the 'if' question to the 'how': *How can the involvement of coworkers create the leadership impact a leader is looking for?*

# HELP FROM COWORKERS MAKES LEADERSHIP EASY

A few years ago, I started a coaching engagement with a new client. Tony had recently been appointed as the regional CEO of a Fortune 100 technology firm. With over 25 years of experience, he had been on a steady climb through the ranks and was now managing one of the top three revenue regions for the organization worldwide. This crucial role brought immense responsibilities and high expectations from the global CEO and board members.

Although Tony possessed extensive international and corporate experience, the new cultures surrounding him presented numerous unfamiliar challenges. He sought my guidance to help him adapt to this environment. As a highly engaged and results-driven individual, Tony aimed to familiarize himself with the prevailing cultures rapidly and to excel as a leader.

Because he had just begun in his new role—and his coworkers were not yet familiar with him as a leader—Tony was unsure about how applicable my coaching would be. Several executives from the organization who had worked with me a few years earlier assured him of the effectiveness of my approach. As we got started, I interviewed the executive team to discern areas for change and the ideal leadership approach for the organization. These insights helped us realize that Tony's primary challenge wasn't based on national cultures. Instead, it pertained to the integration of a highly experienced and multifaceted executive team, one whose members not only had a long career history but solid experience working in

Asia, the USA, and Europe. To manage the organization effectively, Tony also needed to engage with managers deeper down in the organization and grasp their perspectives. So, from being apprehensive about involving coworkers at all, he now wanted to include the extended leadership team of 60 executives in the organization.

As we proceeded to involve coworkers in the coaching journey, Tony gained valuable insights. It soon became evident that the executive team was comprised of specialized and experienced leaders who had been historically undervalued. Optimal teamwork hinged on recognizing these individuals' capabilities and fostering cross-functional collaboration.

Contributions from these team members were diverse. They helped shape an action plan that was both challenging and beneficial, a plan that enabled more effective interactions between Tony and the team, fostering better overall teamwork.

Involving coworkers in the coaching engagement also allowed for valuable input from the next two layers of the organization. This is the part where we reached out to those 60 coworkers, and their suggestions enriched the plan, rendering it more meaningful and relevant to Tony and his executive team.

As Tony proceeded on this leadership journey, he connected his action plan to the business case he had made earlier in the coaching journey. He noticed how everything he was working on was practical, relevant, and outcome-driven. He could see how what had initially felt like a theoretical framework was becoming a robust business case that resonated with the team's needs. And it was the coaching engagement that converted the business case into reality.

Throughout the coaching journey, Tony discovered that he didn't need to change significantly to fit into the new culture. Instead, he found success by being authentically himself, by being open to being vulnerable, by trying new things while allowing others to be genuine, and by being genuinely caring for people. Tony's openness and vulnerability allowed for more effective connections and a positive impact on individuals and the team.

This coaching journey reminded Tony of his past experiences working in various cultures, particularly in China and the Middle East. Whereas people often emphasize cultural differences, he had learned that treating people in the way they feel respected—regardless of culture—leads to success.

This symphony of involving coworkers in the coaching process brought life to Tony's leadership style and the organization as a whole. His genuine care for and dedication to the people he worked with, paired with a collaborative and customized action plan, laid the foundation for meaningful growth and success. By treating people with respect, regardless of the cultural context, leaders like Tony can create harmony and success in any organization.

In the meantime, Tony has moved on to his next (and even bigger) global role and has fully embraced coaching and the involvement of coworkers in his leadership style. And from the executives who work with him, I often hear how much they enjoy this experience, as Tony's approach gives them room to flourish and fly.

# INVOLVE YOUR COWORKERS IN THE LEADERSHIP JOURNEY

In this chapter, we'll discuss the role of coworkers and how they can help leaders improve their leadership effectiveness—quickly and together.

You're going to learn how the cocreation of change actually works. Keep in mind that coworkers have a vested interest in having a better leader, and that coworkers really want the leader to work on things that matter to them. You'll see that the coworkers become the real coaches and advisors in the process—by providing ideas and suggestions for change to the leader.

The coach is more of a facilitator in the change journey, fostering the relationship between the leader and the coworkers and helping the leader convert coworker suggestions into 'show-how' actions the leader can implement in their specific work environment. You can think of the coach as a kind of ambassador representing coworkers in the coaching conversation with the leader. In the next chapter, I will provide an example of this when we take a step-by-step look at how the coach works through leadership challenges in the coaching journey.

# OUTCOMES MATTER TO LEADERS AND COWORKERS ALIKE

From an organizational perspective, there are two critical outcomes from leadership coaching.

1. The leader themselves has recognized their improvement in the areas that are important to them and that they have chosen to work on changing. Needless to say, these areas are also important to the team and the organization.

2. The leader's team, manager, and other coworkers perceive the leader as being more effective. This can positively impact the team's effectiveness and the leader's position within the organization. Engaging with the team better will contribute to positive perceptions. Ultimately, all of these factors impact the team's performance. In our coaching engagements, we measure this Triple Win—Better Leaders, Better Teams, and Better Results—and the results are staggering, as you will see.

Most coaching approaches generally deliver the first outcome, where the leader is satisfied and the coach has a good opinion about the leader resulting from the coaching. Research from Harvard University's Institute of Coaching indicates that leader satisfaction with their coaching in the USA, Europe, and Australia ranges between 65% and 75%. Involving coworkers in the coaching process can significantly boost leader and coworker satisfaction, achieving a 95% success rate in the leader's improvements per their assessments. This highlights the importance of aligning the coaching process with coworker involvement. And though this improvement from 75% to 95% is remarkable, it pales in comparison to what I am going to share with you next.

Let's look at the second outcome, which is that the leader is perceived as being more effective by their coworkers. Interestingly, this is often overlooked, but it is arguably more important and more difficult to deliver. It is exactly where our coaching approach comes in and is so successful.

This is the main question the coach and their clients need to answer: *Am I satisfied that 65–95% of my leaders will be satisfied with their coaching, yet only 18% of the coworkers will confirm that the leader's improvement was successful?* If you answer yes and you decide that leaders' satisfaction is more important than that of coworkers, then you do not need to involve them in the coaching.

But if you agree that leadership is truly about cocreating change with coworkers—the approach leaders use in everything else they do in their organizations—and if you want the leader to be perceived as better not only in their own eyes but in the eyes of their coworkers, then involving coworkers is inevitable. Furthermore, involving coworkers in leadership change creates that Triple Win: Better Leaders, Better Teams, and Better Results.

When coworkers are involved in the coaching journey, everything changes. First, leadership improvement success rates for leaders consistently reach 95% as confirmed by coworkers. This is remarkable on its own—because it is the leader whom the coach was specifically brought in to work with directly. Second, what's even more remarkable is that incorporating coworkers into the coaching process results in 95% of coworkers affirming that the leader's improvement has enhanced the effectiveness of the team and collective performance results. More details about these results are shared in Chapter 11 ('Triple Win for the Client').

This is the Triple Win Leadership approach: The leader, the team, and the organization all achieve better results. Involving coworkers in the coaching process can improve relationships, collaboration, team culture, trust, and respect. It can also help accelerate change, making it more natural, integrated, and visible to coworkers.

Nevertheless, it's important to acknowledge the requirements when implementing Triple Win Leadership Coaching. These include selecting the right clients who are genuinely committed to improvement, the willingness of the leader to involve coworkers, and the readiness to measure results convincingly. Implementing GCG Coaching Tools to automate the coworkers' involvement process helps overcome these challenges, leading to better overall satisfaction with the leader's improvements.

So, remember, by involving coworkers in the coaching journey, the percentage of coworkers perceiving the leader as more effective skyrockets to 95%. This represents a more than fivefold increase in success rates, emphasizing the immense value of engaging coworkers to create a powerful, positive impact.

# COWORKERS PROVIDE THE POWER OF CHANGE

So how do you do that? Let's first articulate why involving coworkers is important and why that perception is important. One of the primary challenges for managers is team members' engagement, as it is a crucial factor in employee retention. One of the main reasons employees leave an organization is a lack of engagement by their manager or their manager's manager and not having clarity about the direction their career is taking within the organization.

These problems can be resolved simultaneously when the manager involves their team members and other coworkers in leadership change.

Why are coworkers important? Coworkers play a crucial role in helping leaders improve, as they have a unique vantage point on the leader's behavior and the behavior they *need* from that leader. Additionally, coworkers have a vested interest in having a better manager, because it enhances their engagement. This leads to increased job satisfaction, a stronger commitment to the organization, and the perception of a brighter career path within the company. When leaders ask coworkers for suggestions and involve them in decision-making, coworkers feel valued, empowered, and appreciated, which engages them visibly in other areas of work as well. I have seen many examples of this over the years.

## DIVERSITY AND CULTURE BECOME ALLIES

The first beautiful thing about the leader involving coworkers is that it presents a solution to the challenges around diversity. The leader no longer has to address the full spectrum of diversity. They only need to cater to the diversity of the people around them—their coworkers.

Second, involving coworkers creates an auto-correct for culture. This is true whether it is a national culture or an industry culture, whether it is in a financial service organization or semiconductor company— which have very different cultures than tech, social media, or even consumer goods. This is true from chips in China to social media in Silicon Valley to finance in Frankfurt.

Coworkers provide suggestions to help the leader work on things that matter to the leader and to the coworker at the same time. They are working together; it's their mutual interest to create an effective and engaged relationship. Another reason that coworkers matter to leaders is that they can crowdsource the change. Leaders are busy— something they always let me know—and time is their most precious resource. I say this to time-starved leaders: By involving coworkers, you don't need to invest time. You can crowdsource this to the people around you, and *they* do the work.

# A PERSONAL STORY ON DIVERSITY

Let me share with you a very personal story from when I was working on improving empowerment in Global Coach Group and working with my coworkers and a coach at the same time. Involving coworkers and asking for their suggestions yielded a wide range of ideas. It made me realize how leadership is such a customized, bespoke affair. As you work with your coworkers, you see that different folks require different strokes.

When I asked for suggestions from Daniel, he was very clear about what he wanted in terms of empowerment. He suggested, 'Let's agree on clear objectives of what needs to be delivered, and then let me go ahead and figure out how to deliver the results to which I'm committed. I'll keep you updated and when I have questions along the way I will let you know.'

When I asked another coworker, Emily, about empowerment, she said, 'Be specific about expectations upfront. There's no need to guess how empowerment should work or how we collaborate. I want to know the requirements and goals, along with your approach, given your extensive experience. Once I understand your approach, I'll go ahead accordingly. This helps me explore your process and new avenues to success, ensuring a smooth, reliable journey. That is a big win for both of us.'

To the same question about empowerment, these two people came up with opposite suggestions.

This is just the reality in which leaders operate, but it made me see that, in my action plan, I could articulate different approaches and then use them for different people in different ways. Then everybody is empowered in a way that makes sense to them, feels right to them, and engages them. Overall, I'm empowering people in a way that makes the most sense to me, giving us a trustful process that people are able to execute and I am able to manage. This is the best way to deliver on the success that we have defined together. A leader can manage and work with a wide range of perspectives and suggestions at the same time.

The same holds for how leaders ask for suggestions. It can be done via email, in one-on-one conversations, or in team meetings. All of these channels are acceptable. Some people will send you suggestions via email because they want to think about it and articulate what a good suggestion is, and then send it to you only after they have completed their thinking process.

Some will say, we spend a lot of time in meetings together, so let's do it privately at the end of one of our meetings. Other people will say, let's make this a team event—in our team meeting that we do once a week anyway. At the end of the team meeting, let's make a round robin and ask everybody to provide their suggestions. Doing so gives you a good collection of the various suggestions that people care about.

# FEEDFORWARD BEST PRACTICES

Feedforward suggestions are amazingly effective and offer various advantages over feedback. Because these suggestions focus on what the leader could do in the immediate future (e.g. the next few weeks), they do not judge the leader's past. Furthermore, feedforward suggestions require knowledge about the tasks at hand (e.g. delegation) instead of knowledge of the leader and their capabilities. To ensure a successful leadership coaching journey and get the best value from feedforward suggestions, consider the following tips and best practices to answer questions leaders frequently ask.

## 1. Online feedforward collection using GCG Coaching Tools

By far, the most effective and acceptable way to collect suggestions is to use the online GCG Coaching Tools, which automatically email coworkers and ask them for suggestions. This approach is effective because it allows coworkers to think through their suggestions before sharing them with the leader and articulate why they feel they are helpful for both themselves and the leader. Their suggestions are then collected and used as input for action planning during coaching sessions. These tools are extremely efficient, automating all communication and follow-up with coworkers. As a coach, you can monitor and manage this online. For more information on the GCG Coaching Tools, visit www.globalcoachgroup.com/coaching-tools

## 2. Suggestions are a gift, and you decide if and how to use them

The leader might wonder if they have to use all the suggestions that people provide and if this makes them accountable for implementing those suggestions. The simple answer is no. When they ask their coworkers for suggestions, remember that they are just that— suggestions. It is like receiving a gift. Upon receiving a suggestion, express gratitude by saying thank you. Afterward, reflect on the suggestions and include only those in the action plan that align with the leader's bandwidth and commitment. Leadership does not equate to following every piece of advice provided by coworkers.

## 3. Keep it short and sweet

The leader may choose to ask for suggestions in person; to collect these suggestions effectively, focus on concise and non-judgmental communication with coworkers. For instance, take 10 seconds to ask a coworker for one or two suggestions for improvements the leader can implement in the next 30 days. Once the coworker provides their input, listen attentively, make notes, and simply say thank you. Avoid engaging in a dialogue or expressing opinions about the suggestions provided. Keep it time-efficient; appreciating their contribution makes the coworker feel valued. Not critiquing their contribution means they will likely share more suggestions in the future. The leader does not need to think the suggestion through at this point anyway, so keep it short and sweet.

## 4. Set up short one-on-one meetings

Some leaders send coworkers a short personal message or email to set up a 5-minute meeting informing them of the meeting's purpose and the areas they are working on, e.g. 'involving other people in decision-making.' This advance notice allows the coworkers some time to think before their meeting. Keep the conversation focused and time-efficient, lasting no more than five minutes. Thank them for their input and avoid discussing these suggestions in depth during this interaction. By reaching out personally and creating a safe space for open communication, leaders increase the likelihood of obtaining valuable suggestions for improvement. This approach works particularly well with coworkers who haven't provided enough input earlier.

## 5. Focus on the future task and not the leader

Feedforward suggestions that people provide are things a leader can do in the near future, say the next 30 days. As they are about the future, which hasn't happened yet, it is easier for people to provide suggestions, because there's no judgment involved. Feedback is about the past, and leaders are attached to their own past, so it is much more difficult for them to be neutral about it. It's also more difficult for the coworker to share such feedback, because it easily becomes judgmental.

Feedforward suggestions are also good because they require task knowledge, not knowledge about the person. If the question is, 'What suggestions do you have for the leader to be better at execution?', a person can still have useful suggestions on this, even if they don't know anything about that leader, because they *do* have knowledge of execution.

Both of these two elements—the future orientation and the lack of necessity for knowledge about the leader—allow feedforward input to be non-judgmental.

All this creates a safe environment for coworkers to share those suggestions. And more often than not, coworkers come up with suggestions they will be involved in during implementation. For example, a coworker might say, 'Let's agree specifically on goals that need to be realized. And let's also agree on how the execution will happen so that we have a common path we agreed on. So I know that when I'm running down that path, you're okay with it.' This is a clear suggestion and it helps the leader because the coworker will be doing all this later.

These best practices work well when the leader is focusing on a leadership change that is both really important for them as a leader and for their team and other coworkers. They create joint interest and joint accountability for success, as you will see later in the book. The leadership growth areas are like a bridge that connects the leader and the coworker, and feedforward suggestions pave the road across that bridge.

To make it work, it's important to make it an easy and low hurdle for the coworkers to be involved. Using suggestions, they create a safe space that is future-focused. Again, there is no real judgment—it's not personal because it's about the future. All of this reduces the power distance between the leader and the coworker.

## THE POWER OF COWORKERS AND POSITIVE CHANGE

The key takeaway from this chapter is that help from coworkers is all around and readily available; it makes leadership change easier, faster, stronger, and more relevant for both the leader and their coworkers. Remember, a lot of this is true because coworkers are not just making suggestions; they are part of the implementation team that makes the change happen.

And just stepping back here for a moment, what are the key takeaways from a coworker's perspective? As I have mentioned, it is essential for coworkers to perceive that the leader has changed, but there is more to it than that. Let's step into a coworker's shoes for a minute and look at the steps of the process from their perspective:

1. My manager is trying to get better at empowerment, so they asked me for some suggestions.

2. They incorporate my suggestions into their action plan.

3. Now I'm part of the execution of that action plan.

4. Once it's done, my manager and I discuss and review this.

5. We repeat that every month.

6. This is not just a new initiative with a one-time implementation; it has become our new way of working together, part of our team culture.

7. As I am proactively involved, I am anticipating the implementation of the action plan.

8. This makes it exciting for me to be back at work every morning because I am actively involved in making change visible.

9. I'm also helping my manager to continue doing this well, because it's important to me.

So you can see how focusing on something that's important to the leader and the coworkers helps to create a great action plan, and how involving the coworkers in a safe and proactive fashion helps to execute the action plan. When leaders do this, change becomes visible quickly and results come quickly, too, which is satisfying on all levels.

# CONCLUSION

Over the last chapters, you have been introduced to a fireproof process to make leadership change happen by:

- Making it simple (by helping people focus on two areas for leadership growth that are important to them and their coworkers).

- Making it easy (by giving the structure of a step-by-step process that leaders and coaches can lean on to make that change happen with a 95% success rate).

- Making that change speedy (by having coworkers provide suggestions for the action plan).

We have a whole system set up. In the next chapters, I will show you how to deal with several specific challenges we often encounter in coaching engagements. So, let's jump right into that.

# ELEARNING RESOURCES

Chapter resources and demos are available in your eLearning account. Sign up and access it here: www.globalcoachgroup.com/triplewinbook or email coach@globalcoachgroup.com

# CHAPTER 9

# LEVERAGING CHALLENGES

Creates opportunities for growth

Everybody has a plan until they get punched in the face! During every coaching engagement, I keep this quote from world champion heavyweight boxer Mike Tyson in mind. My coaching plan or the leader's plan gets knocked around a few times during any engagement. How should you prepare to take on such challenges and turn them into opportunities for growth? That is what this chapter is all about. Challenges come in various forms and formats, are often hidden or at least veiled, and have the potential to derail the coaching engagement, bringing it to a grinding halt.

## CHALLENGES CREATE OPPORTUNITIES FOR GROWTH

It is essential that coaches assist leaders in navigating the inevitable challenges of their leadership journey, helping them maintain momentum to deliver the results they have set for themselves. Coaches should teach leaders to embrace the challenges they face and turn them into opportunities for growth.

What sounds natural and straightforward can be easier said than done. I vividly recall an instance early in my coaching career when helping a leader stay on track became a challenge requiring me to juggle coaching skills and support. I had been coaching Paul for five months, almost halfway through his 12-month journey. Paul was the typical high-energy, smart, and committed executive focused on improving 'actively listening and including opinions of others in decision-making.' During the sixth coaching session, he asked me to remove Jean from the list of coworkers to be involved in his coaching journey. According to Paul, Jean was not genuinely engaged in his leadership development, and her lack of involvement would negatively affect his results down the line. Paul hinted that Jean would probably not mind being removed.

I kind of panicked; Paul's manager had insisted that Jean should be involved as a coworker, and I worried that the issue might make the whole coaching process fall apart. I reminded Paul that he had selected Jean, who was part of his team, and I asked him to revisit his business case, where he outlined the benefits that all coworkers would receive as a result of his coaching. Then I posed this question: Would including Jean in the coaching engagement help her experience the benefits he had listed in his business case, even though he felt she was not as invested in his leadership development as he was in hers? This made Paul realize that it was his role as a leader to commit to his entire team, including Jean.

I had a follow-up question: Would Jean more easily recognize the benefits Paul was providing her—actively listening and including opinions of others in decision-making—by involving her in the coaching journey? And would her periodic reflection on Paul's progress be more accurate with or without her involvement? It then became clear to Paul that involving Jean would make all of this easier, for two reasons: 1) his earlier commitment to involving his coworkers in the Triple Win Business Case he had created, which reflected his investment in his own ideas, and 2) his genuine willingness to demonstrate change to all of his coworkers.

This is just one example of how coaches can address challenges by turning them into growth opportunities. Because challenges like this one occur more often than not, I wanted to find ways not to be caught by surprise and have to find the right solutions on the fly; therefore I build responses to these challenges into the coaching journey. I'll be sharing the most pertinent ones with you in this chapter.

# WHY DO SOME LEADERS GET STUCK WHEREAS OTHERS DON'T?

After facing challenges with different leaders, I discovered that the issues they presented were often similar. So I started categorizing these problems to devise ways to help leaders create solutions for these issues early on in the coaching engagement. This approach not only helps leaders commit to resolving their challenges; it also fosters their personal investment in the solution—because they created them themselves.

Discussions with other coaching colleagues didn't provide the appealing and practical solutions I was hoping for. Based on what leaders shared in our conversations and my personal analysis of the reasons behind their stories, I identified some reasons why they got stuck.

## The main reasons leaders get stuck

1. Leaders often declare victory too early, feeling they've made the necessary changes, but people around them don't necessarily perceive the same level of impact.

2.  Leaders give up due to a significant change in their organizational environment, providing them with a reason (or excuse) to throw in the towel.

3.  Leaders feel that change is a lot of work, and the results don't come as quickly as they had expected.

4.  Leaders feel that coworkers are not collaborating enough to help them change more effectively.

Then I analyzed my successful coaching engagements, whose leaders had faced the same challenges as those who got stuck. What could the stuck leaders learn from the more successful ones? What had the latter done to get unstuck—or avoid getting stuck in the first place? I identified the following solutions that successful leaders applied:

1.  Keep the big picture in mind and persist in the leadership change process until the end, pushing through difficulties along the way, much like a marathon runner.

2.  Be very good at crowdsourcing challenges and solutions to coworkers and lean on their support when the going gets tough.

3.  Stay committed to the promises you made to yourself, your coworkers, and the coach, pushing forward when times are hard.

Here are two general conclusions I came to by looking at this in a 'big picture' way from a coach's perspective:

1. **Reverse-engineer success.** To get unstuck, leaders need to reconnect with the solutions they had devised themselves and apply them to their current problems. These solutions include the Triple Win Business Case, as well as a commitment to we-centered behavior and cocreating change with coworkers. By proactively creating the solutions together with the leader early on in the coaching engagement, the coach ensures a smooth and effective path to success.

2. **Leverage their commitment to their own solutions.** Leaders value their own great ideas and tend to stick to them. This psychology should be built into the coaching journey to anchor positive commitment early on. When leaders are faced with problems, they can bring more of their experience, intelligence, and holistic thinking into the conversation to produce high-quality solutions in a relaxed, constructive environment *prior* to any challenges arising. Creating commitment and buy-in to these solutions from the leaders early in the coaching engagement makes it easier to maintain momentum when you bring them back into the conversation throughout the journey.

Of course, this approach is not unique to coaching—similar principles are applied to things like contingency planning or even holiday travels. But by leveraging the philosophy of preemptive problem-solving and commitment to the journey, you can help ensure successful outcomes. Rest assured that the approaches presented in this chapter have been proven to work time and time again with the many leaders I have coached around the world.

# PUTTING THEORY INTO PRACTICE

There are two adages that are very applicable to our current subject. One is 'In theory, practice and theory are the same. In practice, they are different.' The other one is that when leaders are working on change, 'There is no change in the comfort zone, and there is no comfort in the change zone.' These quotes are from Yogi Berra (one of the most successful baseball players of all time) and top coach Tony Robbins, respectively.

Many of the challenges the leader faces relate to not being comfortable in the new environment they are creating for themselves and their team. They are used to working in their comfort zone, relying on existing structures enforced by their organization's culture or 'Standard Operating Procedures'. Unexpected challenges are now added to their leadership agenda during the coaching—and leaders have little appetite for adding more to the mountain of challenges on their leadership agenda already.

That's where you come in as their coach. The leader can rely on the coaching structure you provide because they know that structure has been proven to work. It gives them assurance that they will succeed in times when they are not in their comfort zone. I found this out by trial by fire. When these challenges occurred, my heart started racing the first few times, and I felt palpably uncomfortable, fearing that the coaching engagement would derail. Stumbling my way ahead, I pushed through some of my ideas to get the leader back on track. Consistently, two realizations popped up in these situations.

**First, I needed to understand the problem behind the problem.** During my MBA problem-solving classes many years ago, I learned to ask questions and let people explain what their problem looks like and what other issues or assumptions have contributed to it. Applying this approach in coaching sessions gives you 5–10 minutes to think about what the problem really is, which solution to bring back, and how to solve the challenge together.

**Second, leaders are typically highly committed people who want to stick to the decisions they made earlier.** Their strong egos do not allow them to contradict themselves in front of you, their trusted coach. They want to get the results they set out to achieve and be recognized for it.

After having these 5–10-minute discussions, I would bring them back to their Triple Win Business Case, Commitment to We-Centered Behaviors or agreement to Cocreate Change with Coworkers, and they would come around rather quickly.

At that point, the conclusion becomes straightforward: First, reverse-engineer these initial solutions to ensure their value for the leader and strengthen the leader's commitment to them, ensuring strong buy-in. Second, bring these solutions back into various coaching conversations over time in a casual and consistent manner.

This approach serves two purposes: Often, challenges never become significant because the leaders quickly recognize the solutions they need to apply. However, if these problems do become challenging, presenting these evergreen solutions back to them quickly helps them redirect their efforts toward the direction they have committed to.

Taking this approach worked better for me than I had expected. Leaders always like their own solutions best. Since they already have a solution to the problem that is now in their vista, it's very difficult for them to deny that a good solution already exists. They just need to do what they said they would do.

# LEAD WITH COURAGE THROUGH ADVERSITY

That is precisely what happened with Joanne in my next example of a leader wanting to exclude certain coworkers. I was coaching the head of HR of a global manufacturing firm—a very smart, experienced, well-educated, hardworking, amazing professional. Her coworkers' list had 15 people, including CEOs from eight countries. She was very committed to involving them.

One of the coworkers was the CEO of their business in Australia, the largest in the region. He was very negative toward Joanne. A lot of it was fueled by internal organizational politics. He didn't like Joanne becoming more successful and powerful in the organization. He felt she was putting his leadership in the spotlight in his own organization, which was officially part of her role as head of HR.

In one coaching session, Joanne said, 'Can we do the coaching without Lucas from Australia? It would be easier without him, and I could still do what I was doing to change as a leader, getting ideas from my coworkers. We'll have enough great ideas without him.'

This was my response: 'Yes, Joanne, we can do that with or without Lucas. Without a doubt, you would become more effective in the eyes of your coworkers. But there are two scenarios to consider, as well as how each of these will impact your leadership journey in the next six months and likely beyond.

'Scenario one is you focus on better HR business partnering and communication. You ask your 14 coworkers, including your manager, for suggestions, leaving out Lucas. Based on their input, you'll make an action plan. We'll do that for six months and measure your progress. I'm sure the results will be great.

'Your leadership growth pulse report will also end up on your CEO's desk. He will say, "Joanne, I see great results. Most coworkers say you got better, and that's fantastic. I can attest to that as I have seen some of these results as well. However, I heard from Lucas in Australia that HR business partnering and communication are still not going well, and he still sees ineffective leadership behavior from you as you work with his team. HR alignment is not happening at the same speed and quality in Australia as elsewhere. And Australia is one of our most important markets, as you know."

'In scenario two, you involve Lucas, the same as other coworkers, and ask them for monthly suggestions. Lucas might or might not provide good ones. You make an action plan and share it with everyone, including Lucas. Then, after six months, when we do another leadership pulse, Lucas will likely see that you are getting better. If not, we still have a report that includes everybody *but* Lucas saying that you have improved your HR business partnering and communication.

The report goes to the CEO and he'll say, "Joanne, it is a great report. I see that you have gotten better and coworkers see that too, which is fantastic. I also see Lucas in Australia still doesn't admit that. Despite the strain between you two, you showed the courage and stamina to involve him. I know that you even included some of the suggestions that came from Lucas in the action plan and it was challenging to implement some of them. Well done, Joanne, and it's sad that Lucas can't move on and see this, too."

'So those are the two scenarios you can set yourself up for. What story do you want to hear from the CEO in six months? Option one, where you got better and excluded Lucas, or Option two, where you improved across the board, even if Lucas might still not admit it?'

Reflecting on that, Joanne said, 'You're right—it will be challenging, but I need to commit to coworkers, and if I do, I'll come out gloriously. Lucas is smart. He likely won't suggest anything bad or undermine me openly. I don't have to accept his suggestions anyway. It will be challenging and tense, but he'll likely be surprised by my resilience in including him. Let's give it a shot—there's a lot of upward potential and little downward risk. Thank you, coach.'

The story didn't end there. Joanne achieved significant positive changes during the first six months of coaching and chose to share these results not only with her CEO, but also with Lucas and several other executive team members. As head of HR, she wanted to lead the way. This made Lucas reflect on his approach and involvement in Joanne's leadership journey.

Although the pulse report data were anonymous, Lucas knew which results reflected his perspective. He had to admit to himself that Joanne had genuinely been doing an excellent job trying to get better at HR business partnering and communication. Over the next six months, as coaching with Joanne continued, Lucas's attitude and working relationship with Joanne evolved.

In the final leadership pulse report, Lucas gave Joanne a thumbs up, recognizing her increased effectiveness as an HR business partner and her improved communication with him and other HR colleagues in Australia. This victory was hard-won but undoubtedly rewarding for Joanne.

The solution I used as a coach was simple: The leader had committed to cocreating change with coworkers (and achieving measurable change). Joanne committed to this upfront, so it's a process she'd embraced already. Building on this, I extended the commitment to the future and helped her see the bigger picture: If she includes Lucas, she will come out stronger despite his negativity. That creates a leadership moment based on doing what's necessary for success, even if it might be uncomfortable.

## UNVEIL SOLUTIONS USING THE LEADER'S FRAME OF REFERENCE

Let me start with an example to put this in context. As part of our coaching approach, the coach conducts individual discussions with coworkers to understand the leader's strengths and areas of development. These conversations provide the coach with valuable insights into the leader's organizational context and the quality of their interactions with their manager, team, or other peers. This knowledge extends throughout the coaching engagement, and it can shape critical moments in the coaching journey.

There are times when leaders might deflect coworkers' suggestions. I worked with Miroslav, the CEO of a European software firm, who was very invested in developing his leadership team through open and frequent feedback. However, some of his coworkers, including his COO Anna, mentioned that Miroslav's feedback was not always productive, leaving employees feeling deflated and disengaged for days after a one-on-one feedback session. And they had these sessions with him several times a month.

During the coaching session, Miroslav dismissed Anna's suggestion and defended the importance of feedback in promoting development. He had learned this while working for many years in American IT firms and claimed it had made him the man he is now. He pleaded that open, honest, specific, and frequent feedback was something he held dear and that people knew this. Drawing on my previous conversations with Miroslav's coworkers, I was able to challenge his perspective by outlining the consequences of his feedback on the team's engagement, productivity, and, ultimately, the company's valuation since delayed projects had caused them to miss revenue targets. This is literally what they had shared with me, and much of it had also been shared with Miroslav in his initial feedback report a few months earlier.

I asked Miroslav this question: 'What is more important: providing the amount of feedback you think people need to have based on your beliefs, or regulating that feedback to ensure high engagement and productivity and to drive the value of your company?' As a major shareholder, company valuation was undoubtedly important to Miroslav, but this need for a balance wasn't something he had considered before.

Upon reflection, Miroslav realized that while he believed he was doing people a favor by providing them with abundant feedback, he might also be depriving himself and others of a solid company valuation. This revelation prompted Miroslav to decide on a course correction, which became part of his action plan.

Taking coworkers' views and acting as their ambassador, coaches can bring real-world insights from previous conversations into the coaching session, giving the leader a fuller perspective and prompting them to reflect on their actions. By turning theoretical concepts into real-life implications, coaches can help leaders realize the potential impact of their decisions and adjust their action plans accordingly.

This powerful approach came into play when I coached Jonathan, who was focused on improving his empowerment skills. Jonathan's coworker, Rose, suggested that he clarify the overall goals to be achieved while allowing her team the autonomy to decide on the course of action for the project assigned to her. During the coaching session, Jonathan dismissed this suggestion by claiming that Rose lacked the necessary experience and skills to understand how to outline and plan her project and task effectively. He did not want to run the risk of failure.

I followed up with Jonathan by asking him a series of carefully crafted questions drawing on what I had learned in my interviews with Rose a few months prior. By highlighting Jonathan and Rose's differing professional backgrounds, personalities, and working styles, I was able to inquire about the potential for friction and inefficiency within their working relationship. Jonathan pleaded his case, and I shared Rose's possible reactions and how they would impact her engagement and commitment to the project.

The coach stepping into the role of ambassador for coworkers offers invaluable insights and real-life discussions, helping the leader see the impact of their decisions and contemplate various solutions. The approach challenges the leader in a constructive way based on actual experiences rather than hypothetical considerations. This is an effective approach for promoting self-reflection, awareness, and growth.

By addressing genuine concerns and exploring options with leaders, coaching encourages positive changes in both their leadership journey and the overall work environment for their team. Ultimately, these changes foster increased effectiveness, engagement, and alignment with the organization's objectives.

## REVEAL SOLUTIONS THROUGH ENGAGING STORIES

I was coaching Veronica, the Regional CEO of a large FMCG organization. After six months of hard work, they launched an updated personal care product for children. The innovation had a huge impact on their production lines throughout the company. They were adapting what was already successful in some other countries, so it was a relatively low-risk but high-impact scenario they were preparing for.

Nonetheless, within two weeks of launching the new product with much advertising fanfare, moms complained on social media that the products were causing discomfort for their children. Of course, this hugely impacted the business revenue, brand image, users, retailers, and other parties involved.

So Veronica called an emergency executive team meeting to discuss the situation, listen to everyone, and make the right decision. An hour into the meeting, they had completely reviewed the situation, and she decided to recall all the product stock back to distribution centers, ship out old products to refill the system, stop new production, and retool the factory for the old product again.

This multimillion-dollar decision was made rather quickly—a huge, bold leadership moment with 70% team agreement and 100% commitment behind Veronica. I took note of this story from our first session because I suspected it could be useful later.

And yes, a few months later, Veronica had an issue with a stakeholder—her manager's manager—who undermined her credibility and confidence. The stakeholder wanted to replace some executives in her team and critiqued Veronica's proposed business strategy.

In our next coaching session, Veronica complained for 30 minutes about feeling unsupported by her management and undermined in her CEO role. She asked what the right solution was for this precarious situation. I remembered her product recall story from our first session and asked how long it took to make that painful but correct decision. 'Less than an hour,' she said. I said, 'Using that same logic here, what do you need to do in this case?' She jumped out of her chair, pointed at me, and said: 'You're right. Let's devise an action plan together right now, because the situation will not change unless I act on it.'

As you coach, keep an eye open for stories leaders or coworkers share that you can use later in coaching conversations to create momentum around action plans, structure, the business case, gaining help from coworkers, or measuring change.

# BE PREPARED TO LEVERAGE CHALLENGES

The key takeaway is that many coaching challenges may be new to the leader but not to the coach. There are recognizable patterns. Utilizing a structured process allows the leader to create high-quality solutions early in the engagement for challenges they might encounter later. Being intentional in articulating these solutions and listening intently to stories from both leaders and coworkers is crucial. Then, when challenges arise, attentive listening and asking questions help the coach understand the real problem behind the perceived one— and then apply the solutions or lessons from their stories to guide the leader forward.

It is critical to focus on results—the leader improving and coworkers perceiving that improvement. The overarching objective is to achieve impact, which we will discuss in the next chapter.

# ELEARNING RESOURCES

Chapter resources and demos are available in your eLearning account. Sign up and access it here: www.globalcoachgroup.com/triplewinbook or email coach@globalcoachgroup.com

# CHAPTER 10

# PERCEPTION IS REALITY

As coworkers vote with their feet

No leader wakes up vowing to make everyone's life miserable at work. On the contrary, most leaders want to improve the lives of their team. However, in the evening, coworkers can feel that it was another challenging day at work that did not improve their engagement. Let's put some numbers around this.

There are two persistent and telling statistics. The first is that less than one-third of employees and managers in most organizations in the developed world are actually engaged (Gallup Global Workplace Report 2024); the second is that two of the main reasons employees leave an organization are a bad relationship with their manager and the team culture. These facts have remained rather consistent for the last 20+ years, which is both sad and troubling, especially in an age where companies need more and better leaders faster to deliver on their strategy.

This situation is not only disheartening for the individual employees who become disappointed and leave the organization—and remember, the best employees tend to leave first, likely for a competitor—but also disappointing for the leader and the company that has invested in them. The cost of bad leadership and low engagement is enormous. Gallup estimates this cost to be USD 8.8 trillion annually (9% of global GDP).

At the end of the day, sorry, at the end of every day, perceptions held by coworkers are the reality the leader is operating in, as challenging and complex as this might be. That's what leaders have signed up for.

The good news is that a leader can change that perception within 6 to 12 months with a 95% success rate; in doing this, everybody wins. The coworkers feel more engaged, the leader is seen as more effective, and performance increases. Again, that is what our Triple Win Leadership Coaching is all about: Better Leaders, Better Teams, and Better Results, with a 95% success rate confirmed by coworkers. I'm sure you have realized by now that this has become an important purpose in my life.

This chapter explains exactly how to get to this perception change in a simple, easy, and time-effective way. Let me take you back to Chapter 8, where we talked about the two critical outcomes important for leadership coaching:

1. The leader recognizes their improvement in areas important to them, their team, and the organization.

2. The leader is perceived as more effective by their coworkers, positively impacting how the leader is embedded in the organization.

The first outcome is delivered by most coaching approaches. The second, being perceived as more effective, is often overlooked, yet it is more important and more difficult to deliver.

Because you are either winning people over step by step or losing them.

I want to look at four quotes. I've heard each of them many times. Combined, I think they take on a whole new meaning.

*No leader is an island.*
*Perception is reality.*
*What gets rewarded gets repeated.*
*You can only manage what you can measure.*

That is, in essence, the challenge we need to face.

Do you recall my earlier example of soft drinks, whose customers vote with their feet? I made a parallel with coworkers and how they vote with their feet as leaders improve.

While change is often simple, it's not always easy. The same goes for having coworkers notice and be satisfied with that change. In this chapter, I will share with you how to make perception change both simple and easy.

The key to success in perception change lies in a leader cocreating change with coworkers on two levels. On the first level, the leader involves coworkers by asking for suggestions, incorporating those suggestions into their action plan, and demonstrating that they are actively working on them. The second level requires reflection, specifically, the leader asks coworkers to review their progress every couple of months.

## A PERSONAL STORY OF CHANGE

I'll share a personal story of what doesn't work, which was a hard lesson for me. Many years ago, when my kids were young, I was a busy regional CEO, and I traveled a lot, so it was challenging to spend time at home with family. I vowed that when I was in town, I'd be home for dinner three days a week. I did this for three months and tracked it, proud of my improvement and assuming that my family had noticed my amazing improvement as well.

One dinner, I asked if they'd noticed a change. They looked puzzled. After an awkward silence, I explained what I'd been doing. When the laughter subsided, they politely said they saw some change but weren't sure how sustainable it would be. That was a hard lesson. As a leader/father, I wanted to create lasting change and make it part of our family culture. But I saw that my change system had three shortcomings, three things I hadn't done correctly.

1. Meaning – Behavior important to me and my family.

2. Involvement – Bringing attention to the change by asking for their suggestions.

3. Perception – Asking for feedback on the changes to see if they had noticed and were satisfied.

## WHEN PERCEPTIONS DO (NOT) CHANGE (TWO TALES OF TWO LEADERS)

Seemingly small differences in your coaching approach to leadership change make a huge impact.

By involving coworkers in the change process, asking for their suggestions, and regularly seeking their feedback as you review progress, you can make perception change more straightforward and accessible, fostering a collaborative environment for continuous growth and improvement.

I'll share the examples of Barry and Beth, colleagues and project managers working toward becoming more effective leaders and being recognized for it.

## Perceptions are resilient

Barry was known as a hard-driving project manager; he was keen on getting things done and exhibited great discipline in implementation. He had little tolerance for people not delivering on promises. While most people on his project team were great collaborators and experienced professionals, two individuals triggered Barry emotionally. This led him to become visibly upset during meetings, occasionally going off the handle and launching into a rant. Barry knew this wasn't the right approach as a project leader. However, he felt his professional reputation was at stake, as he had made specific project commitments to the project owners. He felt that the bad behavior of these two team members would reflect negatively on the whole team and might seep into the team culture.

Barry had some serious discussions with his manager, who wanted to invest in him and support his development. The manager's aim was to see Barry grow within the organization and eventually become a top-level project leader or even a program manager (that was the career journey Barry aspired to). The manager suggested that Barry initiate a coaching engagement. Barry embraced this opportunity, committed to changing his ways, and started 'Project We'. With the support of a senior leadership coach, he focused on 'managing his emotions more effectively in communication.'

This is how Barry and his coach approached his coaching.

Barry was good at soliciting suggestions, incorporating them into his action plan, and sharing the plan with coworkers. At around the 10-month mark in his coaching engagement, an important project was undermined by two team members consistently missing due dates over a six-week period. The entire project was now threatened with major delays, not just affecting Barry but the whole team. The once-secure yearend bonuses now hung in the balance, and Barry knew the team would be very unhappy about this situation.

During a team meeting, Barry singled out the two project team members and reprimanded them for their actions. Both defended their position, explaining why they couldn't fulfill their earlier promises. This touched a sensitive nerve for Barry. He turned red, pounded his fist on the table, and raised his voice, shouting at the pair. In no uncertain terms, he made it clear that their behavior impacted every single person on the team, their bonuses, and how the project's success would be perceived by top management.

Even though Barry's rant was brief, it was undoubtedly memorable. Everyone in the meeting fell silent, and shortly thereafter, the meeting ended. Not surprisingly, the very next day, Barry's manager called him into their office to discuss the incident. The manager pointed out that all the coaching to improve his emotional management in communication had not achieved its intended results. Barry's inability to change had not only made the manager unhappy but was likely to generate pushback from other managers in the organization about Barry's larger projects in the future. Barry had put his manager in an extremely difficult position. The manager shared with Barry that they thought teaching an old dog new tricks might be impossible; perhaps that proverb was true after all.

## Perceptions can change

Beth worked in the same company for the same manager on similar projects. She shared some of the same people from Barry's project teams, most notably the two troublemakers. This is how Beth and her coach approached her coaching.

Beth was adept at soliciting suggestions, incorporating them into her action plan, and sharing the plan with coworkers. She kept her action plan at the forefront during every meeting. It was printed on a sky-blue piece of paper; everyone knew it was her leadership change action plan, and she kept it always visible. During the monthly one-on-one meetings Beth held with her team members, she always spent five minutes discussing her action plan and progress around managing her emotions more effectively in communication. Beth used this time to listen, take notes, and express gratitude for their valuable input.

Every three months, Beth's coach sent out a short online pulse survey asking all team members, her manager, and a few other coworkers to review Beth's progress in her leadership growth area and rate their satisfaction with improvements made in her leadership, their team effectiveness, and project performance results.

Beth had so far conducted this pulse survey twice during her coaching engagement and had openly shared the results with her manager. They would use their one-on-one meetings to review her leadership pulse survey findings and include her coach in these review meetings. The feedback so far had been overwhelmingly positive and had included clear suggestions for further development. Both Beth's coworkers and manager were satisfied with her improvement and the subsequent impact on the team's effectiveness and project outcomes.

At around the 10-month mark in her 12-month coaching engagement, an incident similar to Barry's happened. An important project was undermined by the same two team members consistently missing deadlines over six weeks. The entire project was now threatened with major delays, not just affecting Beth but the whole team. The once-secure yearend bonuses now hung in the balance, and Beth knew the team would be very unhappy about this situation.

During a team meeting, Beth singled out the two project team members and reprimanded them for their actions. Both defended their position, explaining why they couldn't fulfill their earlier promises. Beth had had enough of them, and she became visibly upset. Her demeanor changed, she slammed her laptop shut, and she raised her voice, shouting at the two. In no uncertain terms, she made it clear that their behavior impacted every single person on the team, their bonuses, and how the project's success would be perceived by top management.

Even though Beth's rant was brief, it was undoubtedly memorable. Everyone in the meeting fell silent, and shortly thereafter, the meeting ended. Not surprisingly, the very next day, Beth's manager called her into their office.

But the ending of this story takes a different turn. Beth's manager mentioned hearing about the incident in the previous day's meeting. Various people from Beth's project team and their managers had sent emails and messages describing the incident in sometimes colorful detail.

Beth's manager started their meeting by acknowledging that over the last 10 months, Beth had made significant progress in her coaching and leadership development journey. Beth had not only shared and discussed her action plans with her manager every month but had also shared her quarterly leadership pulse reviews, which corroborated the improvements observed by the manager and others on the team. Even some of the project owners had noted Beth's growth in effectively managing her emotions. While the manager admitted that the recent outburst was not helpful, they maintained that Beth had demonstrated significant improvement in managing her emotions in her communication. The manager labeled the incident as an isolated 'bad hair day' and warned Beth that they expected pushback from other managers regarding her next career moves.

The manager advised her to double down on her leadership development journey for the next two months since, at yearend, everyone would have the opportunity to review Beth's final leadership progress over the past 12 months. Although the incident might come up in the report, her manager believed that Beth's other achievements would overshadow it. The manager encouraged Beth to be aware of the situation and to ask for any help needed to address it specifically.

By doing so, they could clear the road for the success of Beth's project and next career steps.

## Reflection changes perception

These two scenarios are steeped in the reality of coaching and leadership change. Despite the similarities, there are distinct differences, and they are critical to creating the required perception change for leaders and their coworkers. Both examples share a focus on leadership growth, with coworkers providing suggestions and leaders creating shared action plans—a great start.

The main difference is that Beth specifically sought feedback from her coworkers while implementing her action plan, allowing them to reflect on her progress. Additionally, every three or four months, Beth's coach arranged a short online feedback process that resulted in a leadership pulse review report. These reviews required coworkers to evaluate their satisfaction with Beth's leadership growth, its impact on the team's effectiveness, and the project results. Repeated reflection prompted coworkers to keep recalibrating their opinions about Beth's leadership and assess their role and accountability in supporting Beth's transformation. Sharing these reports with her manager provided insight into her progress, further establishing her coworkers' perception of their level of satisfaction with Beth's improvements and how those improvements had impacted the team's effectiveness and performance. When the incident occurred, coworkers viewed it as an isolated occurrence or temporary setback. They believed they would see Beth bounce back soon.

The key to perception change from a coworker perspective involves focusing on two leadership growth areas, gathering suggestions from coworkers, and following up every 3–4 months to measure satisfaction with improvements in the eyes of the coworkers. Measuring their perceptions as part of the progress review should assess the coworkers' satisfaction with the leader's growth on three levels: becoming a better leader, fostering a better team, and achieving better results.

# THE STRUCTURE OF PERCEPTION CHANGE

At the end of the day, the quality of the leadership service that the leader provides is determined by coworkers' perceptions. They are at the receiving end of the leadership service: the eye of the beholder. CEOs of international hotels, marketing directors of fast-moving consumer goods companies, and corporate public relations executives have repeatedly pointed out how our approach to coaching includes similarities to their process of service quality improvement, marketing communication, and public relations. The same clients emphasize the importance of a structured and proactive approach to managing perception change.

Curious about their approach, we aligned our coaching approach further with the known and trusted processes that large companies use in their marketing, business communication, and service quality management.

This resulted in the following structure. I put it alongside a rough outline of the approach many of our clients are using. Here is the step-by-step process:

| The Structure of Perception Change | Communication & Service Improvement | Triple Win Leadership Coaching |
|---|---|---|
| Announce your intentions | Select your audience. Clearly communicate what you plan to do and how this will benefit them. | Select coworkers and define leadership growth areas that are important to them. |
| Share action plans and updates on implementation progress | Share the action plan, and while executing it, keep your audience informed of the progress, confirming that you are following through with your initial intentions. | Share the action plan with coworkers, involve them in the implementation, and bring progress on the plan back into the flow of work during follow-up meetings. |
| Highlight achievements | Showcase how their input and your continuous efforts have led to an enhanced experience or service. | Appreciate their involvement and pinpoint achievements along the way. |
| Continuously improve | Implement the audience's suggestions, and consistently refine and enhance your services or approach based on feedback and the quality of results. | Ask coworkers for suggestions, reflect on your progress, update the action plan, and share it with your coworkers. |

| Share improvement results | Keep your audience informed about the overall progress and improvement scores, showcasing how their input and your continuous efforts have led to an enhanced experience or service. | Measure progress using the leadership growth pulse and share this with the leader's manager. |
|---|---|---|

By following this step-by-step process, leaders can maintain transparent communication, effectively engage with their coworkers, and foster a culture of continuous improvement and growth as they cocreate change with coworkers.

# COCREATING CHANGE IS WORTH IT 10 TIMES OVER

Coaching is appreciated by leaders who take part in such journeys, and managers and companies undoubtedly want to invest in the development of their leaders—but at the end of the day, results are all that matter. Companies invest in coaching to get a return on their investment. It is important to know which results the client is looking for.

Is the organization investing in coaching leaders to improve and engage them? If so, what matters is the leader's satisfaction and their opinion about their improvement outcomes. Focusing on the leader's perception is very relevant when the leadership growth areas are things like self-awareness and self-management, with issues like work-life balance, stress, and mental resilience coming to the fore. It is relatively easy to attain a 75+% satisfaction rating by leaders and a return on the coaching investment of 100% under such a scenario.

A coaching objective of simply supporting the leader is often easily and effectively achieved. However, in most cases, objectives are broader, and clients want leaders to be coached in a way that ensures their team, manager, and possibly other coworkers see improved outcomes. When we talk to clients, these are some of the challenges they want addressed (a complete list of frequently selected leadership growth areas is available to you via our online resource section):

- Engaging team members more effectively to improve satisfaction and increase productivity.

- Enhancing the leader's skills in conflict resolution, fostering inclusiveness, and improving decision-making.

- Promoting diversity and encouraging the team to be more assertive.

- Improving clarity and openness in the leader's communication.

The main point here is that if the outcomes for the leader AND the team or other coworkers matter, then we need to measure results based on their perceptions, in addition to the perception of the leader.

Though this is still simple, if less easy, we have a proven success rate of 95% in measurably improving leaders, teams, and their results.

Clients easily see a return on investment ranging from 100% to over 10,000%, as the benefits extend not just to the leader but to all coworkers impacted by them. This creates a 10–100X return on investment. (You can download various case studies from our online resource section.)

Changing the perception of the leader's behavior in the organization might be more difficult, but it is more important, and thus more *valuable* than just changing their behavior.

So, why do leaders come to work with good intentions, yet their coworkers don't feel the intended impact and leave disappointed at the end of most workdays? Well, leaders are there to engage teams and deliver performance, right? However, the top reasons people leave jobs are *relationships*—with managers, their manager's manager, and coworkers. The engagement leaders want to create with coworkers is undermined in the process of delivering performance. This is understandable: Work revolves around solving problems, so leaders and coworkers are often in challenging situations working to resolve issues. Technology has helped us solve problems faster— which means that we just move on to the next problem faster. And if you think that AI will be the solution, I am afraid that the opposite is true. We will just continue to be involved in more complex problems faster.

Our coaching approach—in which leaders cocreate change with coworkers—resolves these challenges. As the leader improves, the team improves, and organizational performance improves. It's a Triple Win for the client, so everybody wins.

# CHANGE NEEDS VISIBILITY AND IMPACT

Later in my coaching career, I refined how to connect these principles with the clients' organizational context:

1. *Involvement* – Work on what's important with coworkers, cocreate change together, and make the change visible to them.

2. *Consistency* – Maintain change so that new behaviors become new habits embedded in the culture.

3. *Impact* – Get periodic feedback on how coworkers perceive the impact of change.

Then it is rinse and repeat, to make work life better for all.

Research studies conducted globally by PWC, Marshall Goldsmith, and Global Coach Group, involving over 100,000 leaders and their coworkers, have yielded some intriguing findings. When leaders get coached without involving their coworkers, between 75% and 95% of the leaders report satisfaction with their personal improvements. Interestingly, only 18% of their coworkers confirm their satisfaction with the leaders' progress. Conversely, when coworkers are actively involved in the coaching process, a substantial 95% acknowledge a successful improvement in the leaders' effectiveness—a more than five-fold increase. Moreover, this inclusive approach doesn't just enhance individual leadership effectiveness but also elevates team effectiveness and performance results, with 95% of all coworkers, including leaders and managers, reporting significant enhancements.

# ELEARNING RESOURCES

Chapter resources and demos are available in your eLearning account. Sign up and access it here: www.globalcoachgroup.com/triplewinbook or email coach@globalcoachgroup.com

# CHAPTER 11

# TRIPLE WIN FOR THE CLIENT

## Everyone Wins

Leaders typically advocate the power of teamwork. The secret to success in any organization lies in fostering a culture where Together, Everyone Achieves More. This is the essence of the TEAM acronym, promoted in countless workshops and seminars. In today's diverse and dynamic organizational environment, leaders and organizations face numerous people challenges, including finding ways to improve leadership and team effectiveness, employee engagement and retention, and overall productivity and results.

Our Triple Win Leadership Coaching, which embodies a commitment to cocreating change with coworkers, effectively addresses these often-conflicting demands, offering a comprehensive solution. Our years of experience, along with the amazing results achieved with leaders all around the world, make this evident to us—but that conviction is also supported by the data, examples, and case studies shared in the previous chapters.

Addressing challenges at top or mid-level leadership levels in ways that permeate every layer of the organization can lead to phenomenal outcomes. Once again, 95% of coworkers confirmed the improved leadership, team dynamics, and results achieved when leaders cocreate change with their teams using our coaching approach. Time and time again, the results speak for themselves.

Most organizations acknowledge that some of the main reasons employees leave are due to their relationship with their manager or team members or the lack of a clear path for their continued development. Here's a powerful insight: If leaders become more effective in their role and help their teams work together to attain better performance results, most employee engagement and retention issues will be resolved. Imagine your manager regularly asking you for suggestions on how to be more effective and actively involving you in creating and implementing an action plan. Wouldn't this consistent 12-month effort, leading to meaningful, visible, and sustainable results, positively impact your engagement and encourage you to stay at the organization? I'm confident it would. In fact, a million leaders worldwide have experienced remarkable success using this coworker involvement approach in their leadership development journey.

The beauty of the Triple Win lies in three key outcomes: Better Leaders, Better Teams, and Better Organizational Performance. Triple Win Leadership Coaching offers invaluable benefits for leaders and their teams:

- *Better Leaders:* Our coaching method focuses on important growth areas, leading to visible and sustainable improvements in leadership styles.

- *Better Teams:* Improved leadership results in more engaged, collaborative teams, creating a harmonious work environment.

- *Better Performance Results:* Enhanced organizational performance stems from the synergy between stronger leaders and more effective teams.

- *Coworker Involvement:* In our coaching approach, coworkers are involved in cocreating change, leading to higher trust and engagement.

- *Measurable Progress:* Triple Win Leadership Coaching generates tangible results, with 95% of coworkers satisfied with the progress.

- *Streamlined yet Bespoke Coaching Approach:* Our structured approach allows coaches to focus on delivering high-quality bespoke coaching services with measurable results, ultimately supporting more leaders and increasing their impact.

By implementing Triple Win Leadership Coaching, organizations can anticipate significant improvements in employee engagement, retention, and overall performance. By choosing this approach, leaders, teams, and organizations are part of the Triple Win. So, I encourage you to take the first step and embark on this transformative journey with Triple Win Leadership Coaching today.

Some questions have not been addressed yet, and they naturally become part of the conversation for coaching clients considering our Triple Win Coaching services. Let's talk about the most important questions:

1. How do you start, make your case, and scale?

2. How can you speed up the process to get leaders better faster?

3. How can you accelerate change and make more impact?

# HOW DO YOU START, MAKE YOUR CASE, AND SCALE?

Actions speak louder than words. The simplest way is to start off coaching one or more leaders who are eager to get better and want to make a meaningful impact on their team and performance. Within a few months, results start becoming visible, as we have seen in Pauline's case in Chapter 2, and after six months, you have strong evidence of leadership and team improvement that will further solidify in the months thereafter.

Sometimes, HR leaders take matters into their own hands rather than spending a lot of time convincing decision-makers about how coaching can benefit the organization. Let me share this example of a Chief Human Resource Officer (CHRO) who took the initiative without talking much about coaching.

The CEO of a major European multinational company had exciting news: Their new five-year strategic plan to double their business and improve productivity had been finalized, and all executive team members had signed on and committed to making this plan their new collective reality. Françoise, the CHRO, was one of them; she understood the pivotal role that HR plays by developing leaders to deliver on the organization's strategic goals. She also knew that the only way to deliver on these ambitious goals was to develop more effective leaders. In fact, they'd need to double the number in middle management and up, using better HR processes. Françoise had a passion for coaching and leadership development, and she had recently become certified as a Global Leadership Coach and attained her accreditation from the International Coaching Federation (ICF) in the process.

Françoise decided it was time for her and her team to use the Triple Win Leadership Coaching approach to improve their HR effectiveness, support the strategy execution, and build a business case for coaching. She informed her team of her plan and began to Cocreate Change Involving Coworkers. She engaged me to support her as her coach, guide her and her team, and train the whole team in our coaching approach along the way. She did not want to lose time and momentum.

The process started with understanding the benefits of better HR business partnering. Françoise and her team brainstormed how better HR business partnering would benefit the organization, the HR function, and themselves, both as individuals and as a team. They developed a list of benefits, including better delivery of HR results, improved employer branding, and increased professionalism in the HR function.

Françoise then selected coworkers to participate in the coaching. She involved her direct reports, her manager, and various peers in the executive team responsible for manufacturing, marketing, sales, R&D, legal, and finance. Her manager was supportive and curious about the coaching methodology. So, Françoise explained her plans in an executive team meeting, highlighting her focus on 'HR business partnering' as her leadership growth area.

Seeking suggestions from her coworkers, Françoise asked them, 'For me and my team to be a better HR business partner for you, what can we do for you and your team over the next 30 days that would be valuable for you?' She was pleasantly surprised by the number of suggestions, including some novel ideas that emerged, and she started to notice common themes.

Armed with these suggestions, Françoise developed a monthly action plan and implemented it with her team. Patrick, a recent addition to her HR Leadership Development team, played a vital role in helping her finalize the action plan and follow up on the plan each month using the GCG Coaching Tools. They continued this process for three months, regularly involving coworkers by asking them for suggestions and sharing the action plan with them using the online coaching tools.

To measure her progress on better HR business partnering, Françoise used the pulse survey in the GCG Coaching Tools. The results reflected their hard work and were quite positive. All her eight direct reports noted the improvements she had made and commented on how Françoise had worked hard to implement the change and how she effectively enlisted her coworkers to implement the actions. Coworkers noticed her and her team's disciplined implementation of actions and the relevancy of their contributions to business goals. Her seven colleagues in the executive team had been less involved, as they were busy with their strategy implementation plan, alongside paying attention to running their normal business.

Françoise had written countless emails to share her action results with executive team members. Most coworkers across the board were satisfied or at least somewhat satisfied with the initial results of Françoise's work to improve her HR business partnering. However, there were a few very skeptical peers who did not find the changes impactful enough or found that their sustainability was still in doubt. Interestingly, the CEO was clearly involved and had emailed me a few times over the months to share the changes he was witnessing and his observations.

Proud of their initial progress, Françoise shared the results with her CEO and the HR team separately. Her manager applauded the initial success and encouraged her to continue to build momentum and demonstrate impact and sustainability. He felt that there could be a lot of benefit from this approach—though results and the perceptions of executive team members would be the critical buy-in before they'd consider anything else.

Encouraged by her initial success and the support she got from her manager, Françoise doubled down on her change process. She consistently involved her coworkers, and if they didn't provide timely suggestions, she'd asked for them personally in the various meetings they had throughout the month. As she persisted with her disciplined implementation, she noted that it piqued the interest of various peers. They were really curious about what she was doing, and she noticed that people in their teams were also providing comments about increased and improved HR activity.

With the second pulse, completed after another three months, she saw that her extra efforts were paying off. These results were even better; the satisfaction of her peers in the work that she was doing on improving HR business partnering was catching up with the satisfaction that others had expressed. All coworkers were satisfied with the improvements she'd made as a leader, and they also noted how the team's effectiveness had improved, as well as the performance of the

HR function. Most notably, her direct reports really felt the positive impact of Françoise's initiative and how it had impacted their work. All in all, very good results, and it goes without saying that Françoise really felt that she was making the difference she was trying to make.

Even more importantly, she had created a great case for producing results through coaching, in this case, getting better leaders faster. The only hurdle remaining was to convince other executive members. Armed with the latest pulse report, she sat down with her manager and discussed the results. The CEO saw that this was the missing piece of the puzzle, the key to accelerating the implementation and making his strategy become the reality they all had planned for. He knew that scaling the coaching in the organization would definitely reap benefits that would more than justify the efforts and resources required to get them. He invited Françoise to share the results in the upcoming executive team meeting later that week. When she got to work the next day, Françoise found a luscious chocolate cake on her desk with a note from her manager: 'Thanks for being a great business partner; please celebrate your results with your team.' Françoise was touched by her manager's note and felt that her personal engagement with the organization had reached a new level.

The HR core team was thrilled with the progress they had made, and as they discussed the results together, they noted how their team effectiveness had changed. They felt more accountable and better as a team at improving their HR business partnering across the organization. All the activities they had worked on so hard for the last months had paid off, as others had not only noticed them but appreciated the difference they'd made in their business.

During the executive team meeting, Françoise shared her leadership pulse results with the executive team. Though this put her in a vulnerable position, she knew her colleagues would recognize their comments and contributions. She knew they'd recognize how much her HR business partnering had improved and how each of the executives had benefitted from it. Many applauded her courage in taking the initiative for the coaching and sharing her results so openly. They wanted to know how to replicate this approach for their function, seeing it as a great catalyst for their strategic growth.

Françoise agreed to get started coaching most executives and their teams in the weeks to come while planning for a bigger rollout in the organization. As she had hoped, they agreed to leverage coaching to produce more leaders, better and faster. As she and her HR team embarked on this new journey, they knew they were an integral part of their organization's strategy execution and success.

Through conviction, teamwork, and the effective implementation of the coaching methodology, Françoise and her HR team managed to facilitate extraordinary leadership change and personal growth. Their story stands as a testament to the idea that embracing a coaching culture can have a profound impact on both individuals and organizations.

## HOW DOES DURATION IMPACT RESULTS AND SUSTAINABILITY?

Many clients who come to ask us about coaching their leaders to bring about impact and lasting change do so only after two or three

TRIPLE WIN LEADERSHIP COACHING

years of trying to do it themselves. They often ask if we can do the coaching in 3–6 months instead of 12. This raises a good question: How many months of coaching does it take to change issues that have been around for years?

As a coach, you must work out if the challenges you are trying to address with your leaders are recent or have been around for the last few years. When you probe a little, clients often admit that these problems have lingered for some time; after some trial and error with training, assessments, and maybe even some coaching, they have realized that they're not reaping the desired impact. Now, they want coaching that resolves the problem and gets results—quickly.

In these situations, I tell them that it would not be reasonable to assume that a problem that has developed for three years can be resolved in three months. Meaningful impact and lasting results take time.

Additionally, leaders and their managers are generally looking to change the leaders' behavior, which, over time, will become their new habit. This is a process. It takes time before the habit becomes embedded in the team's culture and everybody does it naturally. Only then can there be true short-term and long-term value, making the change sustainable.

Think of diet and fitness, which are not about short-term gains but a change in behavior and lifestyle. This takes time. A team's culture is a product of many years of people working together in certain ways, and making that better takes time. Coworkers want to see that the leader's behavioral change is sustained over a significant period of time, not just for one or two months, and they want to see that the manager is committed to keeping that change moving forward. Only in this way can it provide them with the impact they seek. By taking time to make change stick, everybody wins. So, it is worthwhile to make that long-term investment.

After three months, we can ensure that leaders have both the awareness and the acceptance of what they need to change. After that, action towards achievement starts. After six months, the initial change results become visible. The leader and coworkers acknowledge that the leader has changed their behavior and is on the right path for increased effectiveness—and they can see how it starts impacting the team.

But coworkers want more improvement. They want to see that these behaviors are here to stay and are settled into new habits by the leader and their team. After nine months, the leader and coworkers acknowledge that new capabilities have been embraced by the leader and that it is working for the team. Overall, coworkers are satisfied with the new habits that are in place. At this point, coworkers want to ensure that the change is anchored in the culture and proliferates to the team—they want to see that this is 'the way we do things around here.' After 12 months, the leader has demonstrated the ability to create lasting change, and 95% of coworkers confirm that the improvements in the leader's effectiveness, their team's effectiveness, and performance results are a success. At this point, the leader and the team acknowledge their achievement, something they have never done before and perhaps doubted they could do. All our client results point exactly in that direction. Longer coaching drives more success.

**Longer coaching results in 51% better results confirmed by coworkers after 12 months versus six months of coaching.** After six months, 63% of coworkers recognized the leader's improvement in their selected growth areas due to the coaching. After 12 months of coaching, more than 95% of coworkers clearly acknowledged the leader's improvements as a result of coaching. That is a 51% improvement in satisfaction.

**Longer coaching more than quadruples the number of coworkers being highly satisfied after 12 months versus six months of coaching.** Even though coworkers definitely notice results after six months, only 16% of coworkers are very or extremely satisfied with the improvement the leader has made—and they want more. After 12 months, that number has more than quadrupled to 65% of coworkers being very satisfied or extremely satisfied (an increase of 300%).

**Longer coaching results in 66% more managers confirming the success of coaching after 12 months versus six months of coaching.** I frequently hear from managers that they lack details on how effective their leaders are in working with their teams. Conversely, leaders frequently explain to me that their managers do not recognize all the great work they do with their teams. After six months, 56% of managers confirm that leaders have become measurably more effective as a result of their coaching. And after 12 months of coaching, 93% of managers confirm the leader's improvements as a result of coaching. That 66% improvement makes all the difference for the manager and the leaders.

**Longer coaching results in 61% more coworkers acknowledging improvement in overall leadership effectiveness across the**

**board.** The coaching focuses on two leadership growth areas, but leaders, coworkers, and managers typically want more, and coaching offers the opportunity for much more change. In Chapter 6 ('Focus Changes Everything'), we saw a scenario in which the coach and the leader, based on the feedback from their Triple Win Business Case, outlined a broader benefit picture of the impact the leader wanted to make. After six months, 59% of coworkers confirmed that the leaders' overall effectiveness improved due to coaching. After 12 months of coaching, that satisfaction level went up to 95%, a 61% improvement. This indicates that coworkers are seeing leaders get better not just in two areas but also in other areas that matter to them. So, there has been a significant improvement across the board in coworker satisfaction with their overall leadership effectiveness.

When we look at improvements in team effectiveness and performance results, the numbers are similar.

**Longer coaching doubles the number of coworkers confirming the improvement in team effectiveness.** After 12 months, 95% of coworkers acknowledged the improvements in team effectiveness, whereas at the six-month mark, that satisfaction number stands at 47%. The doubling of the number of coworkers who perceive meaningful improvement in team effectiveness is every manager's dream.

**Longer coaching more than doubles the number of coworkers satisfied with improvements in performance results.** After 12 months, 95% of coworkers confirm improvements in performance results, whereas at the six-month mark, only 42% of coworkers recognize meaningful improvements in results.

These numbers are the sort of fabulous results that leaders work hard to attain with their coworkers. An even better illustration of their success is the verbatim feedback, in which coworkers colorfully share how the changes have impacted them personally and contributed to their professional development and performance.

## MORE COWORKER INVOLVEMENT CREATES MORE IMPACT

Generally, as leaders improve, they want their teams and performance results to improve. We noted a high correlation between more disciplined coworker involvement and leaders, teams, and results improving. This isn't too surprising, but it is an excellent confirmation of how to make the Triple Win Business Case a reality. And this happens quite naturally:

- The leader works to improve and takes coworker suggestions seriously.

- The team improves as coworkers make suggestions that help their productivity and engagement.

- The team has an interest in helping the leader, as it benefits them.

- Because the action plan includes coworkers' suggestions, they recognize the actions and become involved in implementing them. For example, if the leader listens more, coworkers get more airtime. If the leader delegates better, coworkers are delegated *to*, and they feel they have been heard and are involved in the implementation as they perform some of the actions.

As leaders improve, the team improves. With better collaboration, energy goes into moving the business forward—not into more and longer meetings, conflict, and politics. Every effort matters in helping the organization win—clearly, a Triple Win.

The business case in Chapter 6 ('Focus Changes Everything') illustrates how keeping the momentum going like an accelerating flywheel overcomes hurdles and keeps the leader from getting off track. Bringing back the business case when the leader gets stuck embodies the 'why we are doing this and what's in it for me' for both the leader and the coworkers.

The more the leader involves coworkers, the more suggestions they offer and the better these are, which leads to a better action plan and implementation with engaged coworkers. The more coworkers see the change being made, the more the flywheel accelerates. Implementing the action plan, the leader sees that they are impacting coworkers. The traction happens automatically.

Coworkers making suggestions means that they must up their game, too. Change becomes natural; it is integrated into everyone's workflow. A new process and culture emerge—and when it's part of the culture, it sticks, even when coworkers change or the leadership changes.

## WITH THE TRIPLE WIN, EVERYONE WINS

In conclusion, committing to a longer coaching journey in Triple Win Leadership Coaching is a worthy investment for all involved, as it yields significant additional results and satisfaction levels among coworkers. The required time, effort, and investment by the leader decrease proportionally towards the end of the coaching journey, leading to more benefits with less effort. This process is not dissimilar to farming: A lot of work is required at the beginning, and waiting for the right moment to harvest leads to better results with minimal effort.

While coworkers directly involved more readily observe results from the coaching engagement, managers might need more time to recognize and appreciate the leader's improvement outcomes. This is another reason to commit to longer coaching engagements. Along with coworker involvement and a focus on results, these elements will enable leaders, coworkers, and organizations to experience sustainable and measurable growth for themselves and their teams and embed this firmly in their work culture.

# ELEARNING RESOURCES

Chapter resources and demos are available in your eLearning account. Sign up and access it here: www.globalcoachgroup.com/triplewinbook or email coach@globalcoachgroup.com

# CHAPTER 12

# TRIPLE WIN FOR THE COACH

## More Impact, More Coaching, More Clients

# MANAGING SMILING FACES

Like many coaches, I grappled with self-doubt at the start of my coaching career. I questioned my worthiness and skills in helping leaders to face their challenges and improve. Our clients are experienced professionals who understand their own situations, organizational environments, and coworkers much better than an external coach can. That can be intimidating.

As a coach, I worried whether I would grasp their challenges, guide them toward appropriate ideas and solutions, and persuade them to implement action plans and remain accountable. My goal was to deliver value; without that, my impact would be limited, and the coaching engagement might abruptly end.

In traditional coaching engagements, the process typically unfolds session by session, relying on the leader's satisfaction for the next session to be secured. This often leads coaches to manage 'smiling faces', hoping to ensure the leader feels good enough about the coaching to continue.

This 'smiling face' relationship between the leader and the coach quickly becomes a 'pleasing' dependency, a subordinate relationship focused on delivering the leader's agenda. But that often contradicts the requirements of the client, as they are looking for results and an independent collaboration focused on delivering on the wider organizational agenda for Better Leaders, Better Teams, and Better Results. This Triple Win is what clients often really want.

Leaders, client organizations, managers, and coworkers all desire coaching outcomes they can see and feel. They expect leaders to improve and, in turn, positively impact their teams and performance results.

Our coaching service has received exceptional client satisfaction scores, averaging well over 98% of leaders being satisfied with their coach and coaching service. An impressive Net Promoter Score (NPS) of 9 out of 10 and a 74% NPS percentile score places us among the top world-class professional service providers (which are at >50% NPS score). While these scores indicate a very high level of satisfaction, we continuously seek feedback from leaders to improve our coaching service.

Topping that feedback list are the things leaders want their coaches to do more (and better); they include challenging the leader's thinking and assumptions, and adapting action plans. Leaders appreciate being pushed in the right direction and being held accountable for their growth and development. This desire for constructive challenge underscores the importance of adopting a coaching approach that embraces not only supportive guidance but also the courage to address areas requiring improvement openly and effectively. It goes without saying that this runs counter to the 'smiling faces' approach. But it is totally aligned with the Triple Win approach. Of course, when, after a lot of hard work and persistence, the leader gets better in the eyes of their coworkers, management, or other stakeholders—with results to back it up—the smile of the leader becomes big indeed.

By understanding and acknowledging their feedback, we can continuously enhance our coaching service to meet the evolving needs of leaders and organizations. Providing a balanced combination of support and challenge is crucial to driving measurable results, improvements, and lasting progress for both leaders and their teams.

To address these challenges early in my career, I changed the structure of my coaching service. I incorporated measurable outcomes and guaranteed results, and I established fixed-term coaching engagement durations of 6, 9, or 12 months. The leader, their manager, and HR agreed to the coaching terms, creating a structured, results-driven dynamic throughout the coaching service.

This structure transformed the coaching engagement. No longer was I simply managing 'smiling faces'. The focus shifted toward pursuing measurable results, with the leader, coach, and coworkers working collaboratively toward shared goals. I could represent the interests of the coworkers as their ambassador in coaching conversations with the leader. This made it much easier to challenge the leader in their thinking and assumptions and in creating their action plans during coaching sessions. This typically included some tough sessions, in which I challenged the leader to redirect their approach according to coworkers' suggestions. However, it has always positively impacted their leadership growth pulse results every quarter. Leaders who committed to the entire journey were grateful to see the impact they'd created through the eyes of their coworkers in their teams.

Having fixed-term, results-driven engagements in place makes it challenging for leaders to discontinue their coaching after a less comfortable session, and this has given me the courage and conviction to become a better coach for the leaders I work with. I have learned to put aside the need to manage smiling faces and prioritize providing valuable guidance and challenge to my clients as they need it.

I'm sure that if a leader's smiling face were the only success factor, I would have been let go from several coaching engagements. Some leaders have told me, months or even years later, that they felt genuinely challenged and upset during certain coaching discussions, but they ultimately appreciated the confrontation. They needed the pushback I provided to recalibrate their personal convictions and deliver on what their teams required. They thanked me for challenging them, holding them accountable, and helping them change for the better, even if it was difficult at the moment. This always reminds me of most of my experiences at the dentist: It may be uncomfortable and even painful at times, but the long-term benefits make it worthwhile to visit the dentist regularly.

By maintaining my focus on both supporting and challenging leaders, I have come to realize that the most significant growth often stems from moments of discomfort and pushing someone beyond their comfort zone. This approach ultimately leads to more effective and meaningful coaching relationships, allowing leaders to achieve their full potential and positively impact their teams and organizations.

By adjusting the coaching structure to include measurement, guaranteed results, and predefined durations, I changed the nature of the coaching service. This approach allowed me and my clients to concentrate on achieving meaningful outcomes, ultimately leading to more impactful and fulfilling coaching experiences for everyone involved.

When I present quarterly results to leaders, and they see that 95% of their coworkers confirm that they improved, their team's effectiveness increased, and results got better, that brings a genuine and very big smile to the leader's face. I know, as a coach, that the coworkers are smiling too, which they articulate in the quarterly pulse report. These are the meaningful outcomes we all strive for, creating a positive and lasting impact on everyone involved. By focusing on measurable progress and fostering open communication, we ensure satisfaction and growth for leaders, their teams, and the organization as a whole.

At the end of the day, you need to choose whether it's you, the coach, who puts a smile on the leader's face, or the leader's own improvements (acknowledged by coworkers) that do it. I choose the latter any day of the week because that is a true, impactful, and long-lasting result that the leader will relish for a long time. And it's more gratifying and meaningful to me as their coach. Everybody wins. And that's how the Triple Win is structured: Better Leaders, Better Teams, Better Results—and better for the coach too.

## RESULTS SPEAK LOUDER THAN WORDS

In my corporate career, before I started out as a professional coach, I learned that results speak for themselves. Many early clients were results-focused, and many of them echoed the old saying, 'As CEO, you are only as good as your last quarter.' This applies to us as coaches too: You're as good as your client's results—and those results become your brand. Here's an example that opened my coaching eyes.

Early in my career, the CFO of one of the largest electronic companies in the world engaged me to coach some of his peers and other executives to help them improve as leaders. As it turned out, most left their positions around the end of our engagement as part of succession planning—freeing up positions for high potentials. This was not an objective of the coaching engagement; it just happened to turn out that way. After coaching several leaders, I would get comments like, 'Most people you've coached have left—does this mean I'm next?' This became the brand associated with me and my coaching in that company, which affected how my engagements and these leaders were perceived.

The key learning here is to define the brand you want to be known for. Do you want to be known for helping leaders succeed in their current organization and move up while their manager and coworkers sing their praises? Can you avoid being labeled as a different brand (in my case, as the 'transition coach')? Whatever happens as a result of the coaching, whether you caused it or not, influences your coaching brand.

# BUILD YOUR REPUTATION ON CLIENT SUCCESS

As you have seen from the example above, your leaders and their results build your brand. Through some defining experiences, I decided to build my coaching brand based on clients' success, including coworker satisfaction. The involvement of coworkers has proved to be crucial in coaching success.

As coaches implement their coaching service and leaders undertake their leadership development, some of these common coaching challenges inevitably surface:

1.  The excitement wears off, and the engagement fizzles out, which negatively impacts the leader's satisfaction and perceived value of the coaching and the coach. Leaders tend to say something like: 'The coaching was very illuminating at the start. I learned lots of new things about myself and my leadership. But over time, this wore off, and fewer lightbulbs lit up in the coaching sessions as we proceeded, and we ran out of things to explore. It started really well, and it was a good experience, but toward the end, the added value for the coach was not there anymore.'

2.  Though leaders are satisfied with coaching, if coworkers are not involved (as I shared in Chapter 8, 'Help is All Around'), only 18% of them will agree.

3.  Leaders get stuck. How do you get them unstuck? This is one of the biggest challenges, and of course, as a coach, you might have a lot of experience to share with the leader. I have found that leaders know the intricacies of their situations much better than I do. Their arguments against my advice or the resources I share can easily unravel any of my own arguments, making getting them unstuck a huge challenge. It is my opinion versus theirs as they decide on their next steps.

4.  Leaders create great plans, but how do we hold them accountable for implementing them and creating the intended impact? A great

plan only has value once the implementation has been completed and the results are evident.

Again, how you help leaders through these challenges impacts your brand and status as a coach. Here's the story that launched my successful trajectory. We've replicated it thousands and thousands of times since.

A CEO invited me to potentially coach a talented leader he had personally hired. The leader had grown tremendously in 10 years and could have eventually succeeded the CEO, but the leader was too competitive—he thought he knew how to make everything better. He was often right, but people didn't like his way of doing things, and some good people left the organization, which the CEO didn't like. They tried many things, including executive training programs, feedback, and coaching. The results weren't satisfactory enough. Could I make a sustainable change to impact him and his team? It would be a lifesaver for the leader and resolve a major headache for the global CEO.

I proposed my Triple Win Leadership Coaching—involving coworkers, quarterly measurement, a risk-reverse fee model guaranteeing results over 12 months, or pay-as-you-go shorter programs over six to nine months. This was the first time I included the results guarantee in my proposal to a client. The CEO chose the 12-month guaranteed option at my highest fee ever. It took courage to start that journey, and it was hugely successful. We've replicated, refined, and scaled it since then. This book shows you exactly how to do that.

# BUILD TRUST INTO YOUR BRAND

As a coach, you want to be a trusted service provider. This means you need to provide a coaching approach that clients can trust to deliver trusted results. 'Trust' was used a lot in that sentence on purpose. Coaching has been perceived as an opaque service proposition, one that is not clearly defined upfront and has unclear outcomes. Any service whose clients cannot understand how it unfolds or what results will come will not be a great success. And that does not bode well for the perceived value of coaching.

Clients look at coaches as professional service providers similar to consultants and legal advisors or HR advisors engaged to solve a problem. Having grown up in the corporate world, I have aimed for our Triple Win Leadership Coaching to provide trust in results and service delivery.

Easy to say, harder to implement, perhaps. So, I consulted many experts on creating:

1. A transparent service that organizational leaders recognize as they see the parallels with other processes they use in their organizations.

2. Measurable results that solve clients' problems.

3. Guaranteed results so clients don't need to contemplate risk and experience only rewards.

4. Coaching credibility based on value for clients.

The principal partner in a leading European marketing consulting firm pointed me to the work of Dr. David Maister. This was a game-changer. Maister is a former Harvard Business School professor and bestselling author. In his book *The Trusted Advisor*, he explains the trust formula.

The essence of Maister's trust formula approach is that a trusted service is the sum of the credibility of the advisor, in this case, the coach; plus the reliability of the service to address the issue and produce expected results; plus the quality of the relationship that the coach has with the client (e.g. intimacy). That total trust sum is divided by the coach's self-orientation or self-interest. This means that a great coach, with great service, great results, and a great connection with the client, produces great value, provided there is low self-orientation by the coach (which means that the results are not decided, judged, or influenced by the coach). In our case, the satisfaction around the coaching results is determined neither by the coach nor the leader being coached, but only by the coworkers working with the leader.

That is the essence of being a trusted coach. In Maister's book, his formula looks like this:

$$\text{Trust} = \frac{\text{(Credibility + Reliability + Intimacy)}}{\text{Self-Orientation}}$$

And if you're not into formulas or math, that's fine; the logic is firm. Let me explain how you can apply this to coaching in more detail.

1. **Credibility** is the perception of your expertise and reputation in the eyes of your clients; it is determined by your personal

background, your professional experience, and the domain expertise you bring to the engagement.

2. **Reliability** means that your service fulfills the promises to address the challenges and that such service is delivered via a transparent process and creates consistent results. People can see, experience, and witness HOW the service unfolds and WHAT the outcomes are—and that the service can be replicated. They can see that it repeatedly creates reliable results.

3. **Intimacy** emphasizes the personal and empathetic aspect of the professional relationship. Clients and leaders must feel that they connect with you, that you understand their world and genuinely care about them and their concerns on a personal and professional level.

4. **Self-orientation** relates to your motives, which is arguably the most critical component. Self-interest can erode trust. It's essential to align your interests with the client's interests to ensure trustworthiness. The less the coach expresses self-interest and the more their pursuit of the client's interest is demonstrated, the lower their self-interest score. We have minimized the self-interest of the coach because the results of the coaching are determined by the coworkers; the coach has no vote in determining the success of the Triple Win results.

Let's return to the formula Trust = (Credibility + Reliability + Intimacy) / Self-Orientation.

Most coaches focus their main effort on credibility and intimacy. That's great, but it is only part of the equation. It should not end there. Early on, the challenge for me was creating a transparent coaching service that delivered results every time, with all our coaches using this approach. That basically means that it is risk-free and has a 100% guarantee. We also determined to reduce the self-interest of the coach, which basically means handing over the determination of satisfaction with the service to the coworkers and the leader.

Trust is generated not just by the coach but also by the approach and by the fact that the results are determined by coworkers. With agreement on the leadership growth areas early on, there is full alignment on the coaching objectives by the leader, manager, coworkers, and coach. That also means 100% alignment on what success looks like. This makes it easier for the client to accept the coaching service, but it's also easier for the coach to deliver a great coaching service, because it is not just dependent on the coach; it also depends on the other factors that can be trusted to perform.

The key is finding a simple way to turn the 'Trusted Advisor' approach into the 'Trusted Coaching Provider' approach. Now we had to make this easy.

## MAKING TRUST EASY

After numerous coaching engagements and service design iterations, we developed a trusted service approach comprised of four key stages: Aspire, Focus, Commit, and Grow & Measure.

1. **Aspire:** In this initial stage, the leader and coach work together to envision the coaching journey and define the desired outcomes for both the leader and their coworkers. At the same time, they articulate the commitment it takes to achieve these results.

2. **Focus:** Based on feedback from coworkers, the leader identifies two areas for leadership growth, as well as the business case for implementing these changes in their work environment. This is extensively outlined in Chapter 6.

3. **Commit:** The leader then commits to their chosen focus, business case, and coworker involvement, embarking on a journey to cocreate change with their coworkers.

4. **Grow & Measure:** Throughout their growth journey, leaders create and implement action plans based on coworker suggestions, fostering personal development and progress along the way. During this stage, it's essential to measure how the growth is perceived by both the leader and their coworkers. The pulse measure evaluates the satisfaction levels of the coworkers with the improvement of the leader, the impact on team effectiveness, and the results contributed to the organization.

By following this structured approach, coaches can better support leaders in their development, ultimately leading to more meaningful outcomes and lasting improvements for leaders, their teams, and the overall organization.

Making the trusted service simple and easy was done. The next challenge was ensuring that the results gained from coaching were trusted and impactful. We discovered a strong correlation between consistently involving coworkers and achieving better results. Consistent conversations with coworkers, embracing their suggestions, and implementing the action plans together proved to be essential for driving better results that were noticed and appreciated by these same coworkers.

Furthermore, we learned that longer engagements, going beyond six months, had significantly higher satisfaction and impact results (as we saw in the previous chapter). In fact, our 95% success rate for one-year coaching engagements makes it very difficult for leaders *not* to improve. As a result, we introduced a 'no growth, no pay' guarantee for 12-month coaching services. Clients only pay if, at the end of the engagement, the leader has demonstrated improvement to the satisfaction of their coworkers.

This risk-reverse fee proposition offers clients pay-as-you-go coaching services for six- and nine-month engagements and makes payment for 12-month coaching contingent upon satisfactory outcomes. While this approach may seem unconventional, it has proven highly effective for a simple reason: Every coworker involved in the coaching journey shares the common goals of the leader's improvement and an impact being made on the effectiveness of the team.

Customer perception is the reality in every service industry. Coworkers hold the key to determining the success of a coaching engagement—their satisfaction with the leader's improvement, increased team effectiveness, and organizational results are paramount. This results-based approach fosters perfect alignment between clients, organizations, managers, leaders, and coworkers, simultaneously reducing potential bias or self-interest from the coach.

The 'no growth, no pay' guarantee for the yearlong engagements also ensures leaders remain committed to the coaching journey until the end because they want to show results. Most leaders are winners in the game of life. So, results matter. For coaches, this leads to longer yearlong engagements at increased fees; and the ability to demonstrate, measure, and guarantee results further increases these fee levels. This approach not only allows coaches to take on more meaningful engagements but also helps them establish themselves as trusted professionals who prioritize the needs and satisfaction of both leaders and their teams. It is a Triple Win for the client and a Triple Win for the coach.

# INVEST TIME WISELY FOR MAXIMUM IMPACT

As I mentioned earlier, when I was starting out, I found that for every paid coaching hour, I needed to spend two (or more) hours on preparation and follow-up tasks between sessions. This is an unsustainable and unscalable situation. I quickly realized the importance of reducing the hours spent outside the coaching sessions so that I could dedicate more time to coaching leaders and engaging in *more* coaching sessions. Spending more time on paid coaching, and less on unpaid administrative tasks and preparation work, is not just better for the bottom line: It leads to better results, more coaching opportunities, and greater impact.

Efficiency fosters client trust. With my lifelong interest in IT, I started to tinker with coaching automation, which has now evolved into the GCG Coaching Tools. These tools enable efficient management of coaching engagements and automate the collection of feedback and suggestions from coworkers, which enriches the session content. They have also reduced the time needed for preparation and follow-ups to 15–30 minutes. With our non-billable hours dramatically reduced, and provided with excellent feedforward suggestions and feedback results, I and other coaches can focus more on delivering high-quality coaching during sessions. This well-structured approach using GCG Coaching Tools saves time while enhancing the overall quality of coaching, leading to increased leader effectiveness and improved team performance.

## THE TRIPLE WIN FOR COACHES

Using this approach delivers an unmatched Triple Win for you as a coach:

### More Impact

You deliver a Triple Win: Better Leaders, Better Teams, Better Results. Our coaches applying our Triple Win Leadership Coaching approach with their clients find that 95% of coworkers and leaders confirm the improvements in the leader's effectiveness, the team's effectiveness, and organizational performance. This might be hard to believe initially, yet the data we shared in Chapter 11 and the GCG Coaching Tools facilitate delivering this Triple Win 95% of the time.

## More Coaching

The feedforward structure provides insights for high-value, relevant suggestions to be used in coaching sessions. Our online GCG Coaching Tools automate coworker interactions so the coach can focus on coaching leaders in sessions to make more relevant progress and improve their action plans. Leaders feel you deliver high value efficiently while facilitating their growth as they implement their change in the flow of work.

## More Clients

As a coach, results are your reputation, and time is your currency. As your reputation grows, more clients start contacting you. You'll need to spend less time on boring tasks and more on delivering results to clients. Our approach and tools can decrease your between-session preparation to 15 minutes and automatically manage follow-ups. This frees up more time to coach and create impact, enabling more clients as your reputation grows. That virtuous cycle is very scalable.

You become empowered to manage the process to create great value for clients and contribute ideas informed by coworker suggestions. This leaves clients with no doubt you added maximum value. Having high assurance of your worth, you can speak more confidently when selling services. Ultimately, you create more impact, do more coaching, and get more clients, like the results I and the coaches in our network get.

At the end of the day, coaches pursue meaning and significance through impact. More impact delivers the Triple Win. And much of that meaning happens in coaching sessions, where coaches want to spend their time.

## Elevating the Triple Win to new heights: Linking leadership success and social impact

On my journey, I've had the privilege to work with many remarkable coaches and leaders. Simon was a highly successful CEO of Australia's largest food company and director of the United Nations World Food Program; he was also awarded the distinction of Officer of the Order of Australia. As a corporate leader, Simon had dedicated his life to steering his organization toward greatness. Under his astute leadership, the company flourished, securing its position among the top organizations in the region. After his retirement at an early age, Simon decided to make an even greater, more meaningful impact on the world of leadership. After my coach training, he embarked on a journey to become an executive coach—not just any coach, but one who would work exclusively with top-level CEOs committed to seeking measurable progress, cocreating change with their executive teams, and making a difference beyond their organizations. Simon has combined his extensive executive experience with our groundbreaking coaching approach diverging from traditional methods. Instead of accepting payment for his services, he requires his clients to commit to making a substantial six-figure donation to a charity of their choice.

The story of Simon, a retired CEO-turned-coach, serves as a powerful reminder that the pursuit of excellence has no bounds. And his results have been astounding. As CEOs and their organizations have reaped the rewards of their growth and development, they've continued to make their charitable contributions even for many years after the coaching engagement ended. With the support of Simon's coaching, these leaders have transformed their organizations on every level, culminating in a significant societal impact. This story shows that organizational success and social impact can go hand in hand. By intertwining leadership growth, business performance, and the betterment of communities, Simon has not only improved the lives of countless individuals but also redefined the very concept of the Triple Win, with lasting implications for leaders and coaches everywhere.

## ELEARNING RESOURCES

Chapter resources and demos are available in your eLearning account. Sign up and access it here: www.globalcoachgroup.com/triplewinbook or email coach@globalcoachgroup.com

# CONCLUSION – EMPOWERING YOUR LEGACY WITH TRIPLE WIN LEADERSHIP COACHING

Congratulations. You have not come to the beginning of the end but are now at the end of the beginning. As you finish this learning journey through the realms of Triple Win Leadership Coaching, it's essential not only to reflect on the knowledge gained but also to gear up for action. This book has been meticulously crafted to support both budding and seasoned leadership coaches, providing you with the framework needed to develop better leaders, improve team dynamics, and enhance performance results. Let's review the pivotal takeaways, reaffirm how they will aid you in your coaching practice, and set the stage for your active engagement using this transformative coaching approach.

## MAIN TAKEAWAYS FROM TRIPLE WIN LEADERSHIP COACHING

1. **Coworker Involvement is Key:** Embrace this paradigm: If coworkers are an integral part of the leader's work environment, they should be integral to the coaching process as well—actively involved and not merely onlookers. Their involvement leads to

heightened engagement and a 95% success rate in measurably improving leadership effectiveness, team cohesion, and business performance.

2. **Focus on High-Impact Areas:** Use feedback from coworkers to identify two areas of leadership growth that are important for your clients, their leaders, and the teams they lead. And outline a wider Triple Win Business Case for the benefits of growth in these areas for the leader, their team, and performance results. This aligns the goals of the leader, their manager, the team, and you as their coach. With everybody focused on supporting success, measurable improvements are within reach.

3. **Feedforward, Not Feedback**: After the initial feedback, focus on feedforward. Future-oriented and anchored in positivity and constructive growth, feedforward suggestions steer away from the judgment of the past and focus on success that the leader and the coworkers can cocreate together. Feedforward is a proactive, non-judgmental approach that supports leaders and teams in developing actionable and forward-looking strategies.

4. **Follow-Up to Measure Impact at Three Levels:** The proof is truly in the pudding: Measurable outcomes reign supreme in any organization. By concentrating on enhancements recognized by their coworkers, our methodology not only measures noticeable results in leader development, team dynamics, and organizational performance but also intensifies coworker engagement through the reflection process. When coworkers actively reflect on the improvements made, they become further engaged; they become active supporters in the cocreation of the

changes the leader is trying to implement. This reflection moves coworkers from passive observers into active participants, as they see the substantial benefits—increased effectiveness, better communication, and stronger collaboration—that also enhance their own work experience. This active involvement generates a cycle of continuous improvement and commitment from all sides, ensuring the Triple Win is not just a goal but an ongoing reality.

5. **Structured and Scalable Coaching Methodology:** Our approach is not one-size-fits-all but a tailored pathway that aligns with individual and team needs, ensuring reliability and scalability in most organizational contexts. This structure supports coaches and their clients in managing more clients efficiently while maximizing impact.

6. **GCG Coaching Tools:** Enhance the effectiveness of your coaching with the GCG Coaching Tools. These tools not only streamline the action plan implementation for leaders but also make it easy to involve coworkers and gather their suggestions, significantly saving time for coaches. Utilizing these tools ensures disciplined execution by leaders, easy participation by coworkers, and efficient management by coaches, all contributing to even better results, with a 95% success rate.

## EMPOWER YOUR PURPOSE

The purpose of this book on Triple Win Leadership Coaching is clear: to equip coaches with the insights, tools, approaches, and strategies to further their coaching success and deliver a Triple Win—Better Leaders, Better Teams, and Better Results. Our approach is designed to support coaches to excel in delivering superior results for your clients and the leaders you coach. These tangible client benefits help you as a coach create more impact, do more coaching, and get more clients. Success breeds success.

# EMBARK ON YOUR TRANSFORMATION JOURNEY

Investing effort and time in yourself and your clients is the key to unlocking the power of Triple Win Leadership Coaching. Taking the next steps forward is easy, and you can choose to do it on your own or join our GCG community, which is committed to your growth as a Triple Win Leadership Coach. Here are three simple ways to get started:

1. Utilize this book and the free resources at www.globalcoachgroup. com/triplewinbook to incorporate Triple Win Leadership Coaching in your client engagements and bring lasting change to their lives.

2. Enhance the coaching journey by leveraging the GCG Coaching Tools to make your Triple Win Coaching engagements even more efficient and effective, achieving a 95% success rate. Harness the power of these tools to meaningfully engage coworkers, leaders, and their teams to improve performance results.

3. Elevate your coaching qualifications by refining your skills through practice and learning and attaining your ICF-accredited certification in Global Leadership and/or Team Coaching. This unleashes your full potential and amplifies your impact on your clients' lives and their coworkers.

For insights, experiences, or inquiries about Triple Win Coaching, contact us at coach@globalcoachgroup.com.

Remember, the journey of a thousand miles begins with a single step. Taking action today means opening up a new chapter in your professional life. Embrace the opportunity to grow, influence, and transform lives—your own and those of your clients and their coworkers. With your newfound expertise, go forward and make an incredible difference!

# EXCLUSIVE OFFER FOR THE FIRST 100 COACHES

Dear Coaches,

If *Triple Win Leadership Coaching* has inspired you to help leaders and their teams achieve measurable improvement, this invitation is for you. If you aspire to coach leaders and their teams to be more effective, with a 95% success rate, I invite you to take a transformative journey and let me personally guide you on the path to accelerating your coaching success.

I extend this offer to you because, on my journey to success, I missed having someone to guide me through obstacles and accelerate my progress. My offer to you is to be that guide. Imagine having access to top-tier training, state-of-the-art eLearning modules, and live workshops where you can practice all aspects of Triple Win Leadership Coaching. You'll even get personal coaching to have all your questions answered. Picture working with your clients equipped with a suite of GCG Coaching Tools and resources designed to deliver measurable and transformative results. This is not just a dream—it's an exclusive offer to make this your coaching reality.

To make this dream come true, take just one step, and all will unfold from there.

**Your step:** Join the Global Leadership Coaching Certification Program.

The Global Leadership Coaching (GLC) Certification Program is your gateway to kickstarting further success in your coaching practice. As you participate in this program and its live workshops, you will learn and practice all aspects of Triple Win Leadership Coaching, receive personalized feedback, and get all your questions answered. Such hands-on experience is crucial to refining your skills and boosting your confidence as a coach. This comprehensive program provides all the coaching resources you need for a lifetime and equips you with all the skills needed for Triple Win Leadership Coaching. By earning this prestigious leadership coaching certification, accredited by the International Coaching Federation, you not only enhance your competence and credibility but also pave the way for your ICF coaching accreditation.

And I will continue to be by your side, adding more exclusive benefits:

## ACCESS TO GCG COACHING TOOLS

As part of this exclusive offer, you will have unlimited use of the GCG Coaching Tools for one year. These cutting-edge tools and resources are meticulously designed to ensure your coaching interventions are efficient, impactful, and measurable, setting the foundation for your client's Triple Win success and your own with More Impact, More Coaching, and More Clients.

## MARKETING TOOLS TO GET MORE CLIENTS USING OUR COACH BUSINESS ACCELERATOR (CBA)

The Coach Business Accelerator (CBA) offers invaluable tools and resources designed to empower leadership coaches to excel in both coaching and business management skills. The course provides a comprehensive framework for building a successful coaching business, emphasizing client acquisition and effective marketing and sales strategies. Participants learn to establish a robust social brand, leveraging social media like LinkedIn to attract and engage potential clients. The CBA also equips coaches with essential marketing techniques, including content creation and email campaigns, to nurture and convert leads into clients. Additionally, the course offers downloadable resources to support continuous learning and application of strategies. By mastering these tools, coaches can increase their client base, enhance their impact, and achieve sustained business growth.

## PERSONAL COACHING AND CONTINUOUS LEARNING COMMUNITY

You will be invited to exclusive monthly GCG coaching online meetings where you can share your personal questions. If you need one-on-one time, we will arrange this separately during or after these meetings. This ensures you continuously learn from others and receive personalized guidance from me.

This journey will ensure you are well-prepared to deliver impactful coaching sessions, attract more clients, and achieve measurable results. By taking the first step, you will be on the path to becoming a highly successful and sought-after coach. Transform your coaching career with the Global Leadership Coaching Certification Program. Register here today: www.globalcoachgroup.com/triplewinbook and use the code TRIPLEWIN100. This offer is limited to the first 100 coaches who register.

Your path to a more impactful and rewarding coaching practice begins here. Let's make this vision your reality.

Let's Lead for Good.

Will Linssen and the Global Coach Group Team

| | |
|---|---|
| Top Executive Coaching Voice | @ LinkedIn |
| Advisor | @ Harvard Business Review |
| World's #1 Leadership Coach | @ Global Gurus |
| World's #1 Coach Trainer | @ Thinkers50 |
| Master Certified Coach | @ International Coaching Federation, ICF |

Chapter resources and demos are available in your eLearning account. Sign up and access it here: www.globalcoachgroup.com/triplewinbook or email coach@globalcoachgroup.com

# Notes

Made in United States
North Haven, CT
28 July 2025

71113290R00146